INTERNATIONAL STRATEGIES IN TELECOMMUNICATIONS

Dealing primarily with the telecommunications industry, this book applies the strategic states model to the international business strategies of industrial companies. Telecommunications is currently a key empirical field as a comprehensive deregulation process is taking place and the bases for competition are changing.

The book provides:

- A broad description of the telecommunications industry.
- Details of an in-depth study of the telecommunications group Ericsson. This includes their development in major markets such as Germany, the USA and Japan.
- A description of how the strategic states model has worked for Ericsson and other companies.

The strategic states model enables us to describe the current state and strategic development of any company or organizational unit. Using this method a company can scrutinize its alternatives and better understand its position and the possibilities for the future.

This book relies on original research and highlights important choices in the development of international business strategies.

Anders Pehrsson is Associate Professor of Business Administration at the School of Business, Stockholm University. He has written several books and has contributed articles to the *Journal of Strategic Change* and the *Scandinavian Journal of Management*. He teaches at universities and works as a business consultant.

ROUTLEDGE RESEARCH IN ORGANIZATIONAL BEHAVIOUR AND STRATEGY

INTERNATIONAL STRATEGIES IN TELECOMMUNICATIONS

Model and applications

Anders Pehrsson

London and New York

First published 1996
by Routledge
11 New Fetter Lane, London EC4P 4EE

Simultaneously published in the USA and Canada
by Routledge
29 West 35th Street, New York, NY 10001

Routledge is a Thomson International Publishing company

Typeset in Garamond by Keystroke, Jacaranda Lodge, Wolverhampton
Printed and bound in Great Britain by Redwood Books,
Trowbridge, Wiltshire

British Library Cataloguing in Publication Data
A catalogue record for this book is available from the British Library

Library of Congress Cataloging in Publication Data
A catalogue record for this book has been requested

ISBN 0–415–14829–4

CONTENTS

FIGURES

TABLES

PREFACE

I found the task of contributing to the literature in the emerging area of strategic management a truly interesting endeavour. It is a rather intricate field of research, as it covers so many different aspects. In my work I have tried to capture the development of international business strategies, which I think is an area not properly understood.

The book relies to a large extent on original empirical research and a combination of research methodologies. Important choices in the development have been highlighted, using primarily quantitative methods and multivariate analyses in the studies. In addition, qualitative methods were applied in the description of the telecommunications industry, and in the longitudinal case in order to get deeper into the relevant matters. This case was initiated in the early 1980s, constituting a part of my doctoral thesis. Since then I have been working on the case which has received an extended treatment in this book.

I would like to thank here all the persons at the Ericsson telecommunications group who were kind enough to invite me for interviews and were open enough in other ways to answer relevant questions and discuss the matters in hand.

Although the results and shortcomings of this book are entirely mine, I am grateful for the discussions with my colleagues, which have pushed the work forward. Thanks are also due to all MBA students at the School of Business, Stockholm University, who helped by applying the earlier versions of the models and discussed the examples.

This work received financial support from Stockholm University. Between 1992 and 1994 I had the opportunity to work part-time on this book and on the underlying empirical studies. I thank Professor Lars Persson who assisted in making this financial arrangement. A study of strategic states and performance applying to Swedish companies in Germany was given financial assistance by the MW '80 foundation,

The Swedish Committee of the International Chamber of Commerce. Another study focusing on strategy choice problems in Germany was partly financed by The Wenner-Gren Center foundation.

Teresa Bjelkhagen provided skilful assistance in proofreading earlier versions of the manuscript and helping to improve the language.

Finally, I would like to dedicate this book to my wife Ann-Helene who has been supportive throughout the process, and to our small children Tobias, Terese and Andreas whose infectious curiosity and energy constituted an extra enticement.

Anders Pehrsson
Stockholm
January, 1996

1

INTRODUCTION

This book presents and applies the strategic states model, mainly in the telecommunications industry. As it is subject to comprehensive de-regulation, the industry is an interesting object for a strategy study.

The model enables us to describe the strategic development of any company or organizational unit and its current strategic state, as well as various alternatives for the future. By using the model, a company wishing to evaluate its establishment on a certain geographical market or to examine any other strategic alternatives for the future has the possibility of better understanding its position.

The strategic states model is based on the contingency perspective. This means that the characteristics of the environment and the organi-zation have decisive influence on the available strategic alternatives in each state. Thus, in each state or position in the two-dimensional space defined by the model, there is a certain freedom of action and an optimum strategy.

Although conceptually oriented research and books applying the contingency perspective in other strategic models exist, the empirical evidence consists primarily of statistical data and superficial case studies. I have tried to contribute to the area of strategic management research by developing and applying the contingency model in the context of international business strategies of industrial companies, and by discussing a number of important choices in strategy development. Empirical examples and a longitudinal in-depth study illustrate strategy developments on international markets. Original research in terms of cross-sectional studies published in international scientific journals constitutes a major foundation for the book.

The book is divided into two parts. The first part (Chapters 2 and 3) discusses central considerations in the development of international business strategies, with examples from different companies and industries. In Chapter 2 the strategic states model is presented in detail. The model follows the contingency perspective of strategy, which means that the environment and the organization constitute the basis for dimensions in which generalized patterns of strategies can be found. Segment penetration, the degree of adaptation and performance are the dimensions used in the model. Divergence, concentration, standardization and adaptation constitute distinct strategic alternatives within the space defined by the dimensions of segment penetration and the degree of adaptation.

The model defines four extreme strategic states. The freedom of action and the most efficient business strategies for reaching high performance are totally different from one state to another, not least due to competition. The four optimum business strategies are characterized by 'volume customers', 'efficient distribution', 'long-term customer relations' and 'order reproducibility' respectively.

An empirical study (Pehrsson 1995a) showing a linkage between strategic states and financial performance is presented in Chapter 2. This study implicitly highlights three important choices of industrial companies in the course of development of international business strategies. Chapter 2 briefly indicates these choices and discusses some normative conclusions. In Chapter 3 the three choices are more thoroughly examined.

The question of penetration of relatively few or a variety of market segments is the starting-point for Chapter 3. To assist in answering the question that may be asked by any industrial company, a theoretical review on market segmentation precedes the case concerning segmentation in Europe.

Second, the type of offer and the corresponding strategy problems are discussed. This section of the chapter is based on one of my articles (Pehrsson 1993) which compares problems experienced by industrial companies marketing mainly separate products as compared to those marketing systems of products.

A study (Pehrsson 1995b) of alternatives when it comes to standardizing or adapting an offer from one market to another is the basis for the third section of Chapter 3. This study focuses on the evaluations of Swedish industrial companies penetrating the Swedish and the German markets simultaneously. Business concentration, product adaptation, and user divergence are explicit strategies that emerge from the referred study. As a conclusion, evaluation of strategic alternatives are discussed.

The second part of the book (Chapters 4 to 6) presents the development of international business strategies in the telecommunications industry. Chapter 4 describes the industry in terms of important changes that take place (the deregulation process and the evolution of mobile telephony systems), and major actors in the industry. Here, both company examples and broad surveys provide information. Chapter 5 presents the Ericsson case. This case follows a longitudinal in-depth approach in which the development of strategies for both the group and single business areas is being described. The business areas of Public Telecommunications, Radio Communications and Business Communications are focused on, as well as the development of their strategies on the major markets such as Germany and the USA.

Finally, Chapter 6 discusses Ericsson's development with reference to the strategic states model. Ericsson's choices imply focus on telecommunications systems and accompanying customization. When it comes to these systems, customer divergence and geographic divergence are present. These strategies manifest, for example, in an effort to establish customer relations with different network operators, and the formation of strategic alliances with other companies in the industry.

Part I

CENTRAL CONSIDERATIONS IN THE DEVELOPMENT OF INTERNATIONAL BUSINESS STRATEGIES

2

THE STRATEGIC STATES
MODEL AND APPLICATIONS

A company's strategic decisions belong among the most important affecting its survival abilities. In the field of strategic management most authors agree that the strategy implemented by a company shows the direction which it has been following for a long period of time in order to survive and reach its performance objectives.

A business strategy for the future is thus a direction which a company chooses with regard to its products and markets, and considering its internal resources and the environmental situation. Different types of issues are involved in the choice of a long-term direction. This applies to the composition and development of the offer and the review of customer categories and their geographical locations.

Theoretically, environmental and organizational analyses generate strategic alternatives that are evaluated and selected (for example, Ansoff 1965; Bourgeois III 1980; Chakravarthy and Lorange 1991; Steiner 1979a). However, a business strategy does not usually develop in a straight line, but through a series of complicated variations, which often appear anything but obvious to the chief actors (Brandes and Brege 1990; Chandler 1962; Mintzberg and Waters 1985; Pehrsson 1985). Considering that many years may pass between the initial idea and the achievement of a significant sales volume of a company, with investigations and judgements going on continuously, a strategy will often have to be constantly revised and developed. In retrospect, a single choice may appear to have been almost random or else to have represented the only available alternative. In either case, a choice is never an isolated act, but an accumulation of previous decisions reflecting a history of traditions and values, as well as the immediate pressures of the necessity for survival. Each decision delimits the freedom of action in strategy formulation and implementation.

Knowledge and understanding of a company's history and emergent restrictions on the strategic freedom of action enable the company to position itself today and to delineate strategic alternatives for the future. Based on my empirical strategy research and literature studies I argue that the freedom of action in business strategy formulation is defined by the structure of the state in which the organizational unit of current interest is situated. Thus, in each and every state there exists a certain freedom of action and an optimum business strategy.

In the strategic states model which I have developed (Pehrsson 1985, 1988, 1990, 1991, 1993, 1995a, b), the environment of a company is reflected in the dimension of the breadth of the market that is being penetrated. The market breadth is measured by the number of market segments that are being focused on, in which a segment is a limited and measurable part of a larger market.

The other dimension is valid for the organization and concerns the adaptation of the offer to the requirements of the customers in the market segments. The offer can be composed of physical products and services in different degrees.

The degree of the company's segment penetration and adaptation decides its sensitivity to variations in price and other competitive means, as well as the possibilities of adaptation to changes in competition or other environmental fluctuations. Hence, the freedom of action varies according to the two dimensions of the model.

In each position or strategic state in the two-dimensional space there is a certain freedom of action and an optimum business strategy. The strategic states model can therefore be seen as an application of the contingency approach to business strategy. The treatment of strategic performance is widely discussed in this perspective, but I prefer to use financial measures such as return on the capital employed or profit margin.

This model enables us to describe the strategic development of any company or organizational unit and its current strategic state, as well as the alternatives for the future. Divergence, concentration, standardization and adaptation represent pure strategic alternatives.

DIMENSIONS IN THE STRATEGIC STATES MODEL

In the strategic states model, the breadth of the market penetrated by a company or any organizational unit is specified by a number of segments that are being penetrated. If the company or unit of current interest follows a divergence strategy and penetrates a larger number of segments than it did earlier, its dependence on the single segment decreases. Concentration means here fewer segments and an increased dependence on each single segment. This is also the case when one or a few segments become dominant in the company's business activities.

A market segment is a limited and measurable part of a larger market. Scandinavia is one geographical segment of the European market, while Sweden could be regarded as one geographical segment of the Scandinavian market. Manufacturers of machines could be viewed as a segment of the manufacturing industry as a whole. In this case it is therefore appropriate to talk about a customer segment or intermarket segment that crosses geographical borders. The concept of intermarket segments is generally defined as the presence of well-defined and similar clusters of real and/or potential customers across national boundaries, showing the same characteristics and being identified by similar criteria (e.g. Levitt 1983; Douglas and Wind 1987; Jain, 1989).

An effective segmentation procedure results in parts of a market which can be identified and measured. The segments should be large enough in terms of customers' purchasing volumes and the potential profitability for the companies penetrating the segments. Equally the segments have to be accessible to penetration and defendable against competition (Pehrsson 1991).

Once the market segments have been identified, they have to be described. A segment can be described either by the demand characteristics of the customers or by the demographic characteristics of the customers in the segment. Jain (1989) extends the description procedure and discusses the general conditions applying to a market segment. He suggests the following three characteristics of market conditions: cultural characteristics, economic characteristics and customer perceptions.

In my empirical study (Pehrsson 1995b), the use and existence of intermarket segments were identified as follows. As segmentation is normally valid for product users and not intermediaries, segmentation concerning the using companies was the focal point of the study:

- demographic characteristics (location of users in terms of industries, size of using companies);
- operating characteristics (users' experience of the product, users' need for after sales services, users' business and technological competence);
- purchasing characteristics (users' buying routines);
- situational characteristics (users' need for quick and safe deliveries, certain product applications, users' normal order sizes);

- competition characteristics (number of alternative offers from which users can choose).

All the above characteristics except the one concerning competition are present in the segmentation model of Bonoma and Shapiro (1983), in which they are proposed to be used for the segmentation of industrial markets. According to the authors, demography is the most crucial segmentation base. The reason for this is that demographic information is most easily available. Demography has also been treated as a segmentation base in, for instance, the study of Sorenson and Wiechmann (1975).

However, since the company that follows segmental penetration rather than penetration of the whole market can be more efficient than its competitors, competition has to be taken into consideration in segmentation. The model of Flodhammar (1977) consists of a competition component in terms of a number of alternative offers from which a buying company can choose.

In the strategic states model an offer is described by the degree of segment adaptation. In this dimension, the development can show increasing standardization or adaptation to the requirements of customers in segments. When it comes to the offer, it can be composed of physical products and services in varying degrees.

The presence of competition may necessitate customization of the product in order to gain an advantage over the rivals, by providing a product which will ultimately match the local conditions precisely. Similarly, if the company's competitive position does not vary depending on the market, pursuing a global strategy may be more worthwhile (Porter 1986). This means that the greater the degree of similarity in the firm's competitive position in different market segments, the higher the degree of product standardization.

Toyne and Walters (1989) suggest that adaptation generally means a significant adjustment of the basic product programme from market to market in order to bring it into line with different customer needs and varied market environments. The basic product programme may be one followed on the domestic market or developed after consideration of explicit needs and situations on foreign markets.

I prefer to use the term 'customization' when referring to the adaptation of the product programme to satisfy fully any customer's requirements. 'Localization' is an appropriate term as regards adaptation of, for instance, the product design to meet the local environmental forces specific to a given geographical market. It usually leads to the development of a diverse collection of product programmes with a limited commonality from market to market. Localizing may be necessary and desirable when the conditions of product use and other important factors differ significantly between the various geographical markets.

Local responsiveness is a related term that refers to resource commitment decisions taken autonomously by a subsidiary, primarily in response to the local competitive demands or customer demands (Prahalad and Doz 1987: 13). In a wide variety of businesses there may be no competitive advantages to be gained by coordinating actions across subsidiaries. Typically, businesses where there are no meaningful economies of scale or proprietary technologies fall into this category. The need for significant local adaptation of products or differences in distribution across national markets may also indicate a need for local responsiveness.

Dependence on market segments and the degree of adaptation in the strategic states model define a company's sensitivity to variations in price and other competitive measures, as well as its ability to make a quick response to changes in competition or in the environment as a whole. Consequently, the company's freedom of action varies in accordance with the two dimensions of the model. At a given point of time, the freedom of action is decided by the structure of the company's strategic state.

The two dimensions can be put into operation in several ways. Measurements should apply, however, for a certain period of time such as, for example, one year. This will facilitate the application of the model in practical situations. As regards segment penetration, this dimension can be operationalized by use of the following variables:

- share of the invoicing for the three most dominating market segments;
- share of the invoicing for the three most dominating customers;
- share of the invoicing for the three largest orders;
- share of the market segments accounting for 80 per cent of the invoicing;
- share of the customers accounting for 80 per cent of the invoicing;
- share of the orders accounting for 80 per cent of the invoicing;
- share of the invoicing for the three most dominating countries.

The degree of adaptation can be operationalized by the use of the following variables:

- average time for a customer project (i.e. average time necessary from the project initiation to the final invoicing – longer time means greater adaptation);

- average time for order execution (i.e. average time from order booking to the final invoicing – longer time means greater adaptation);
- share of the invoicing referring to customized orders, as distinguished from standard orders.

As the list of the variables indicates, appropriate operationalization is influenced by the type of the offer marketed by the company and the type of customers catered for. Provided relevant variables are used, the application of the dimensions should pose no problems.

Information concerning segment penetration during a certain period of time can be gathered from sales statistics, while statistics concerning order bookings and sales give information regarding the degree of the adaptation of the offer.

The efficiency of a business strategy is measured by performance indicators. Although the importance of the performance concept is widely recognized in strategic management, the treatment of performance is perhaps one of the thorniest issues confronting the academic researcher as well as the practitioner. The majority of strategic management theories either implicitly or explicitly underscore the performance implications, since the performance constitutes the time test of any strategy.

Venkatraman and Ramanujam (1986) have shown that financial performance is the type that dominates in strategic models. Typical of this approach would be to examine indicators such as sales growth, profitability, earnings per share, and so forth. The authors continue to say that a broader conceptualization of performance would include emphasis on indicators of operational performance (i.e. non-financial performance in addition to indicators of financial performance). Here, it would be logical to treat such measures as market share, new product introduction, product quality and measures of technological efficiency within the domain of business performance. These measures focus on those key factors of operational success that might lead to high financial performance.

If one adds to the relatively straightforward financial and operational measures all other measures valid for organizational performance in general, one finds that a number of these are contradictory. For instance, actors outside a company will frequently consider the effectiveness of the company differently from various groups of actors within the company.

Although a broader conceptualization of strategic performance is welcome, I think it is the financial and the operational measures that are the most suitable in measuring performance in a strategic model.

As information concerning financial and operational performance is normally available from within a company, I suggest that a relevant financial or operational measure should be chosen in the application of the strategic states model.

DIVERGENCE, CONCENTRATION, STANDARDIZATION AND ADAPTATION

Segment penetration and the degree of adaptation form a two-dimensional space as in Figure 2.1, which illustrates the strategic development of a company during the period from 1989 to 1994 and possible strategic alternatives for the future.

In order to increase its financial performance, the company in the example was trying to concentrate on fewer market segments for the five-year period. Earlier, the company was interested in the whole of Western Europe, whereas in 1994 only Scandinavia was being penetrated. A certain concentration is also valid for the machining industry. In this case, the whole manufacturing industry earlier constituted the market for the strategy that assumed a more divergent character.

The company had been strongly affected by problems concerning cost calculations when offering relatively well-adapted products. The company has therefore standardized its offer to a large extent in order to meet the common requirements of the customers in the Scandinavian machining industry. The present standardization strategy is manifested in the effort to be cost efficient and well prepared for price competition.

The example shows that divergence means penetration of a larger number of market segments and normally also smaller dependence on single segments. Concentration, on the other hand, implies an increased dependence. This is also the case if one or just a few segments become dominant.

The degree of adaptation can be adjusted by the implementation of standardization or by the use of adaptation strategies. Standardization means making an offer more uniform, while adaptation means that it is shaped to suit the unique requirements of customers in various segments.

The concentration strategy could be further implemented by the company in our example. It would then be suitable to segment the machining industry in more detail. The main interest should be accorded to companies manufacturing different types of machines and located somewhere in Scandinavia. Companies in attractive segments will be potential customers of the company.

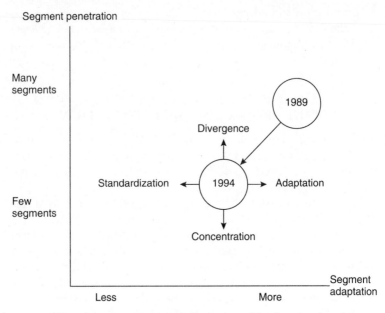

Figure 2.1 Strategic alternatives for a company based on its
state in 1994

The standardization strategy could be even further intensified. In this strategic alternative it is necessary carefully to assess the value of the standardized offer when it comes to the penetration of various market segments. Perhaps the offer, or parts of it, need to be refined.

Divergence is a business strategy for the future that can be appropriate if the financial performance of the company allows it. In this case new customer groups or geographical regions are being sought. New markets for the established products and services will be scrutinized, as well as possible applications of the offer. As the number of segments increases, the company might want to engage distributors to take care of individual customer groups or regions.

As a fourth alternative, a review of the mixture of products and services is conceivable. This is especially valid if the ultimate financial objective has not been reached. A certain adaptation could produce quick results, but it would probably imply a confusion in choosing competitive advantages to emphasize. In order to reduce costs, the company could minimize its own manufacturing capacity and engage subcontractors instead.

14

The strategic development of the Steel Wire company is an interesting example of putting the strategic states model into practice. In the middle of the 1980s the company manufactured and marketed different types of wire, where the raw material consisted of rolling wire produced in rolling mills. The company's production process was organized around stations. At the first station, the rolling wire was refined into simple wire and at the other stations the wire was further refined. As the production machines were inflexible, so that in principle it was impossible to manufacture anything other than wire, the strategic freedom of action was substantially restricted.

The Steel Wire company delivered both to other companies within the group and to external customers, primarily in Scandinavia, but also in Western Europe as a whole. These customers ranged from small companies, which would use wire in applications such as packaging, to very large customers who would refine the wire themselves to be used, for instance, in shelves for refrigerators. Small companies as well as individual consumers would purchase from wholesalers as a rule, while large customers would be in direct contact with the Steel Wire company.

Due to certain investments in a larger production capacity as well as mature market demand in the middle of the 1980s, the company demonstrated significant overcapacity. In this situation the management decided to extend inventories, instead of restricting capacity. This policy resulted in a lower turnover rate of capital. As production investments were mainly financed by loans, the interest burden combined with the restricted capital made the financial situation severe.

However, most of the international competitors behaved similarly. That is, a continued build-up of production capacity was a regular feature at that time. Since market demand remained at the same level, each additional investment in production capacity automatically implied overcapacity in the wire industry. Consequently, with regard to standardized wire, competition focused on price putting a strain on profit margins for competing companies. Foreign low-price competitors rooted in Europe and elsewhere found their way to the markets of the Steel Wire company.

In principle, there existed two ways in which the company could have lowered its prices and yet kept the profit. Either the volume could have been increased, or the costs could have been cut. Given the competition on the market, it was almost impossible to increase the volume quickly. Thus, the only available alternative was to cut costs.

Variant A in Table 2.1 in 1985 constituted the main product of the

company. Costs for raw material represented 85 per cent of total manufacturing costs. This means that lower prices on steel wire and preserved
profit margins demanded lower costs for rolling wire.

Despite a mature Western European market, rolling mills in
countries such as Belgium, Britain, France, the Netherlands, Italy and
West Germany expanded their capacity. On average, the capacity
utilization of a rolling mill was not more than around 60 per cent in
the first part of the 1980s. This strongly motivated them to find export
markets for their marginal volumes. In these efforts, low prices became
the major weapon of competition.

At first sight low prices on rolling wire seemed to be beneficial to
companies like the Steel Wire company. Unfortunately, the large
customers were aware of the decreasing prices of raw materials and it
became very difficult for Steel Wire to lower its prices at a slower rate
than the rate at which the costs for rolling wire were decreasing. In fact,
the largest customers were frequently asking for even lower prices,
which totally destroyed the margins for the wire producer.

In order to survive, a number of rolling mills started to refine their
material into wire products. Considering the huge investments in production and the limited freedom of action, a forward integration was
a logical strategic development. At the same time competition in the
wire industry was further increasing. In fact, in 1985 the Steel Wire
company showed losses and a negative return on the total capital.

The business strategy which was evolved for Steel Wire relied on three
cornerstones: market concentration, customization and integration
(Figure 2.2). Market segmentation procedures showed that the
largest customers were the most attractive and the easiest to reach.

Table 2.1 Manufacturing costs for variants of wire produced by the Steel
Wire company (variant A 1985, B and C 1990)

Cost factors	Variants		
	A	B	C
Rolling wire	85	65	55
Direct wages	2	4	7
Salaries	4	11	16
Electricity	1	5	1
Interests, depreciations	5	7	7
Other costs	3	8	14
Total	100	100	100

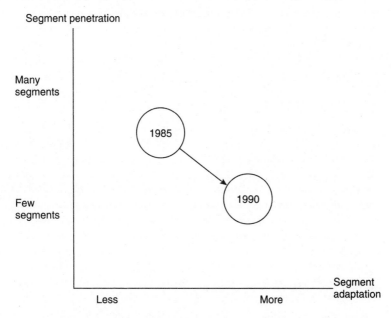

Figure 2.2 Strategic development of the Steel Wire company

Concentration on these customers made it possible to capture a relatively homogeneous product quality and similar delivery requirements. Customization thus consisted in the offering of variants of wire that included more than just a minor refinement of rolling wire. Step by step, Steel Wire engaged the largest customers in cooperation concerning quality, for example, in the context of wire for refrigerators. There was also an attempt at cooperation with rolling wire suppliers in order to increase their quality consciousness.

In 1990 variants B and C were developed and sold to major customers. The value added to the raw material is reflected in the relatively high shares of direct wages, salaries and other manufacturing costs. These costs were applicable to more intense product development and marketing programmes.

As regards business ratios, the turnover rate of capital had increased, mainly due to just-in-time deliveries, smaller production inventories and inventories of end products, as well as decreased accounts receivable. Lower costs were achieved primarily through rationalization in administration and production. Finally, a smaller dependence on the costs of rolling wire facilitated price discussions with customers. In

1990 the Steel Wire company accounted for 15 per cent of total capital return.

A business area, a large company or a company group must often manage in reality a portfolio of businesses, covering a variety of standardized and adapted products. The history of the Swedish company ASEA (now a part of ASEA Brown Boveri) is an example of such a case. Since the 1880s the company has been conducting extensive sales of products that were not manufactured by the company itself (Glete 1983: 50). In the early days this electrotechnical company took full responsibility for entire constructions, while its manufacturing concerned only electrotechnical machines. Even though the manufacturing programme was broadened with time, at the turn of the century ASEA's sales still included products manufactured elsewhere. This applied especially to installation materials.

The sales of 'heavy' products (power and industrial constructions, trams and locomotives), which were extensively customized, were smaller in the 1890s than the sales of standardized products, such as installation materials. However, the share of 'heavy' products was increasing. This dualism and the problems inherent in the balancing of 'heavy' products against 'light' products, of advanced, hazardous construction deliveries against less hazardous deliveries of standardized products, is a characteristic feature of ASEA's history.

After 1903 the company succeeded in creating a sales volume that was large enough to balance possible miscalculations concerning single construction deliveries. This objective was considered to be very important by the company. Earlier experiences had made the management aware of the risks connected with dependence on few deliveries. For instance, in the middle of the 1890s a planned delivery to a rolling mill had to be postponed, putting the future of ASEA at stake.

During the first decade of the twentieth century the share of invoicing for standardized products had increased and reached a peak of 76 per cent between 1917 and 1920. In fact, this was the highest share during the whole period from 1890 to 1980 (Glete 1983: 71). During the 1920s, the proportions of 'heavy' and 'light' products changed several times. However, at the end of the decade standardized products were dominant again reaching a share of 70 per cent.

In the deep recession of the early 1930s, the Swedish authorities demanded electrification of the railway network and, consequently, ASEA's sales of 'heavy' products increased drastically. After this period, constructions dominated ASEA's portfolio and the share of invoicing increased to around 70 per cent.

In the early years of the group, the parent company had a relatively high share of standardized products. But from the 1930s the parent company focused on 'heavy' products, whereas the subsidiaries took care of 'light' products. Subsidiaries were added to the group primarily by acquisitions.

During the period from 1955 to 1980 the 'light' product area of the group contained mainly the parent company's sector of motors, electrical appliances, relays and electronics, together with subsidiaries such as Cable, Sewe-Selfa and Järnkonst. The products of this area could be regarded to have constituted the profitability base of the group, which was also the purpose of dealing in standardized products. The aim was to generate profits and balance the hazardous 'heavy' products, which demanded heavier research and development resources and implied dependence on relatively few customers. On the other hand, many standardized products were sophisticated and could be used in the 'heavy' products and constructions of ASEA. As the group manufactured the majority of the components for its constructions, the dependence on subcontractors was reduced. At the same time the standardized products were sold to external customers.

Figure 2.3 illustrates the strategic development of the ASEA group between 1890 and 1980 in terms of the dualism between 'heavy' and customized products, as compared to 'light' and standardized products. The highest share of invoicing for standardized products appeared in 1920, while the share for customer orders ('heavy' products) reached a peak in 1940.

OPTIMUM BUSINESS STRATEGIES IN FOUR STRATEGIC STATES

One difficulty of the research on business strategy is the fact that two identical strategic settings never occur. This problem has given rise to three approaches to studying strategy: the situation-specific, the universal and the contingency views (Hambrick and Lei 1985).

The situation-specific view sees strategy as an artful alignment of environmental opportunities and threats, internal strengths and weaknesses, and managerial values (e.g. Andrews 1971). Proponents of this view are in favour of case research, maintaining that analysts can draw no conclusions about firms' strategies unless they understand the firms' unique position. Some quantitative research has also demonstrated that strategic generalization beyond one or two firms can be risky (e.g. Hatten *et al.* 1978).

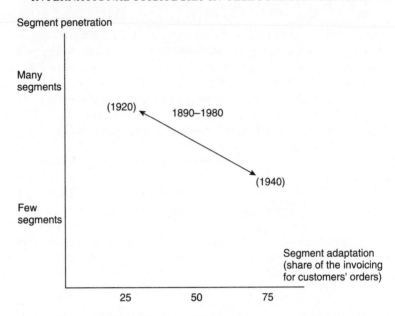

Figure 2.3 The ASEA group's dualism between standardized and customized products, 1890–1980

Hambrick and Lei continue and present the universal view to studying strategy. It is stated here that universal laws of strategy exist and apply to a certain extent in all competitive settings. For example, the Profit Impact of Market Strategies (PIMS) programme popularized the 'law' of market share, implying its universal applicability in the statement, 'there is no doubt that the relationship can be translated into dynamic strategies for all businesses' (Buzzell *et al.* 1975: 102). Given these laws, any business would be well advised to pursue the strategy of aggressive building up of cumulative experience and market share. Such laws imply that there is only one grand type of competitive setting and one universally sound strategy.

The underlying assumption of contingency approaches to strategy (Galbraith and Schendel 1983; Ginsberg and Venkatraman 1985; Hambrick and Lei 1985; Hill 1988; Hofer 1975; Miller 1988; Pehrsson 1993; Steiner 1979b, and others) is the idea that successful business strategies depend on being able to define an appropriate relationship between variables management controls, such as product development, production and investment decisions (Ginsberg and Venkatraman 1985), and those variables which are generally outside the direct control of strategic management. The latter non-controllable variables have been defined as environmental variables (Galbraith and Schendel 1983). These variables consist of market structure, number of competitors, market growth, barriers to entry, and so on. However, the environment could also be divided into sectors, on which management would be generally able to exert some influence. This applies to customers and the technological level of the market (Pehrsson 1985), whereas business climate and competition constitute those environmental sectors which are less controllable.

Hence, the contingency approach means that an optimum business strategy exists, provided certain internal and environmental premises apply to the company. In other words, one assumes a relationship between two independent variables, which influence a dependent variable. The strategic performance of the company would then reflect the degree of its success.

The strategic states model follows the contingency approach. Using the dimensions of the model, it is possible to define four extreme states. The type of competition is totally different in the four states. This means that the freedom of action and the most efficient business strategies for reaching high performance vary from one state to another. Figure 2.4 illustrates the four extreme strategic states, together with the characteristics of the corresponding optimum business strategies.

The relative standardization of products, as well as their concentration by means of the penetration of a limited number of market segments or customers, implies that rationalization and conservative cost control are particularly important. Since customers generally do not perceive any important differences between competing products except for the price, product standardization signifies that price is a decisive competitive measure. High profitability requires that customers within relatively few market segments demand large volumes, which is why the phenomenon known as 'volume customers' is a characteristic feature of the optimum business strategy in this strategic state.

In my survey of thirty-seven West German subsidiaries of Swedish electrotechnical companies (Pehrsson 1995a), the penetration of a relatively low number of customers was indicated by the fact that the share of the invoicing for the three largest orders in 1988 was higher than 20 per cent. In the same year a share of the invoicing for customer orders lower than 60 per cent showed that relatively standardized products were offered. Heat measuring instruments and telecommunication equipment are just two examples of products in the study which can be included in this strategic state.

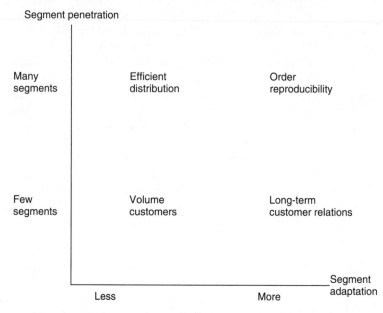

Figure 2.4 Four strategic states and characteristics of the corresponding optimum business strategies

A company's bargaining power could increase by the application of a more divergent business strategy and by offering standardized products to many different market segments or customers without any dominants. Having simple products and numerous customers means, however, that long-term customer relations may be difficult to establish. Such relations normally give a possibility of developing and highlighting competitive advantages other than price, which means that the company's vulnerability to price competition decreases.

Divergent strategies and standardized products imply that it is frequently advantageous to cooperate with distributors or other inter-mediaries that have wide customer contacts. The ability to handle distribution channels will have a decisive impact on company perfor-mance. This strategic state focuses then on logistics and is characterized by 'efficient distribution' as its optimum business strategy. In the West German study referred to above, products such as electronic office equipment, lamps and electric tools were placed in this state.

A higher degree of the adaptation of products and services to the requirements of customers in single market segments makes it possible to create a more unique offer and to be less dependent on price as a competitive measure. Of course, it is still of paramount importance to keep the costs low, even if this may be difficult considering that tailor-made services and subsequent personnel costs are generally more extensive than those concerning standardized offers.

If the products have been highly adapted to just a few market segments, then high risks are involved. First, segment dependence gives a lower bargaining power. In such a case it may be difficult to argue for a relatively high price, notwithstanding the fact that the price does not presumably decide a customer's choice of a supplier. Second, problems with payment or other hardships that the customer must endure might eventually have serious consequences for the company. These would be caused by the dependence and the corresponding restrictions on the freedom of action. Third, as the products are presumably adapted to very specific requirements, they cannot be easily available to customers in other market segments.

On the other hand, adaptation makes it possible to build up long-term relations with customers. In addition to any other benefit, such relations and the accompanying customer loyalties make it possible to create barriers for competitors threatening with low prices. On the condition that costs can be minimized, an effort to create long-term customer relations can generate high profitability in this strategic state. Accordingly, the goal of 'long-term customer relations' is a significant feature of the current optimum business strategy. A supplier of complicated equipment like, for example, advanced computerized systems is a typical representative of this state.

Extensive adaptation to several market segments, requiring different product variants, constitutes the fourth and final extreme strategic state. Although the distribution of risks is usually satisfactory and the chances of reaching high profitability are good in the long term, this state is quite demanding. Since the variation in customer requirements is extensive, it calls for a large and decentralized organization. At the same time the high degree of product adaptation makes it difficult to reach scale effects in production and in other functions. Good financial results are made possible primarily through a search for orders which are significantly similar to each other and, consequently, by trying to exploit the learning effect. Thus, 'order reproducibility' is a distinct feature of the optimum business strategy in this strategic state. Here, large building construction companies working internationally, penetrating numerous customer types and carrying out time-consuming building projects are typical examples.

STRATEGIC STATES AND COMPETITION

Since buyers in principle have a decisive impact, of course, on their decisions of what to buy, by whom and when, competition arises between established industry competitors. These competitors normally have the ability to gain favourable positions by product development, price adjustments or exploitation of other competitive means. Intense competition arises particularly if buyers or customers acquire a high bargaining power in buying situations.

Persson (1990) discusses the concept of competitive pressure and argues that it implicates a risk of unsatisfactory results for a firm. That risk is due to the presence of competitors and will eventually result in unsatisfactory results if nothing is done to prevent it. According to Persson, competitive pressure emerges from:

1 autonomous changes in buyer needs;
2 the appearance of new competitors or products;
3 the marketing behaviour of competitors;
4 changes in costs compared to competitors.

Porter (1980) presents a similar view and states that intense competition arises as an effect of factors such as these:

- many or equally powerful competitors;
- only minor differences between competing products;
- negligible costs for a buyer who chooses another supplier;
- high fixed costs, which requires high capacity utilization;
- difficulties for competitors to withdraw from the industry.

Many competitors in principle imply a rich supply of products that buyers can evaluate and choose from. In this case competition is intense and buyers have a high bargaining power in a buying situation. The situation is even more favourable if existing competitors are equally strong, and no one has the ability to dictate prices and other terms. If products are standardized in nature the evaluation process of buyers is easier compared to a situation where products are more differentiated, particularly if switching costs are negligible.

High fixed costs in an industry generally imply that competitors have a desire to exploit their capacity as much as possible in order to acquire revenues. A common tendency here is a prioritization of high volumes at the expense of high prices, and this type of behaviour might result in overcapacity in the entire industry.

Substitute products or other threats which become realized in a short period of time make the existing products obsolete. If, by reason of superior threats or any other reason, a competitor wants to withdraw from an industry and encounters difficulties in trying to do so, the result will be a larger supply than otherwise and intense competition. Companies investing in industries with high barriers for withdrawal run the risk of being caught by the industries.

Porter advocates that the formulation of competitive strategy in an industry can be equated with choosing the main group of competitors in which to compete. This choice may mean selecting a group which already exists and which involves the best trade-off between profit potential and the cost to the firm for entering it, or it may mean the creation of an entirely new group.

Thus, the first step in structural analysis in industries is to classify significant competitors according to their business strategies. This then allows for the mapping of the industry into strategic groups. A strategic group is commonly defined as that group of firms in an industry which follows the same or similar strategies in certain key strategic dimensions. An analysis of strategic groups is an intermediate step between looking at the industry as a whole and considering each firm separately.

Strategic groups occur for a wide variety of reasons, such as differing strengths and weaknesses between firms, different times for entering the industry, or historical accidents. However, once such groups have formed, the firms in one strategic group will in general resemble one another closely in many ways besides their broad strategies. They tend to have similar market shares and to be affected by and respond similarly to external events or competitive moves in the industry, because of their similar strategies. If, for example, a small competitor reduces its price, competitors in a large company group may select to keep their prices on the same level as before.

The strategic groups in an industry can be represented on a map. The number of axes is obviously limited by the two-dimensional character of the printed page, which means that the analyst must select a few particularly important strategic dimensions with which to construct a map.

For mapping strategic groups, Porter suggests a number of useful principles. First, the best variables to employ as dimensions are those that determine the key mobility barriers in the industry. Mobility barriers deter the movement of firms from one strategic position to another. Different strategic groups represent different levels of barriers, which provide some firms with persistent advantages over others. Second, in mapping groups it is important to select as axes variables that do not move together too much. For example, if all firms with high product differentiation also have broad product lines, then the two variables should not both serve as axes on the map. Rather, variables should be selected that reflect the diversity of strategic combinations in the industry. A third principle is that an industry can be mapped more than once, using various combinations of strategic dimensions.

If we consider previous empirical studies concerning strategic groups, we find that the most evident difference between these studies arises from the strategic dimensions chosen to define the strategic groups. At one extreme the studies are based on single measures, such as relative size (Caves and Pugel 1980; Lahti 1983; Porter 1973; Primeaux 1985). More common is the use of multiple measures. However, these seem to be rather haphazardly selected from a mix of strategy descriptors such as vertical integration and diversification (Hunt 1972; Newman 1978), or from operational or functional strategies such as research and development expenditure, advertising intensity and marketing channels (Dess and Davis 1984; Hatten and Schendel 1977; Hatten et al. 1978). Thus, I agree with McGee and Thomas (1986) that a minority only of previous empirical studies emphasizes detailed knowledge and understanding of the industry context in specifying the strategic dimensions.

In applying the strategic group concept, the analyst must select the dimensions for constructing a map. But this is not an easy task. Unfortunately the researchers have paid no attention to the uncertainty inherent in the selection of strategic dimensions. In my opinion another principle must therefore be added to Porter's three, namely that dimensions must be considered crucial by as many strategic managers as possible in the relevant industry. This principle ensures that the chosen dimensions are distinctive features of the industry and deeply entrenched in the industry context. If there is consensus regarding the crucial strategic dimensions, time-consuming discussions about the choice of these dimensions can be avoided. Such discussions generally arise because managers vary in their perceptions and knowledge of competitors' business strategies (Pehrsson 1985). Differences in perceived uncertainty tend to produce differences of opinion. Consequently there should be as little variation as possible in perceived uncertainty when it comes to identifying the major candidates for selection as dimensions. Perhaps underlying factors may be more appropriate than the obvious variables as regards choosing strategic dimensions? If a few factors only could be suggested as dimensions, then the choice problem could be reduced.

Pehrsson (1990) presents a survey study that seeks to throw fresh light on the concept of the strategic group. Four key dimensions are proposed for grouping competitors according to their business strategies. Thus, competitors could be classified according to the breadth of their market scope and the degree of adaptation to customers. Product quality and pricing can also be used as dimensions in identifying strategic groups. These dimensions apply primarily to analyses in the electrotechnical industry, or parts of it.

Hence, the sample of the referred study comprises 44 Swedish electrotechnical companies. Twenty-four of these compete on the Swedish market and twenty on the US market. Mail questionnaires were used to collect cross-sectional quantitative data about the competitor perceptions of the company presidents. Analysis of the data reveals slight differences only between perceptions in Sweden and the USA. Correlations among variables were also calculated and underlying factors were distinguished. These factors constitute the dimensions for classifying competitors.

The strategic dimensions can be used for several mappings of competitors. In applying any pair of dimensions, however, the analyst should check that the two values of the pair do not move too closely in the same direction. When it comes to mobility barriers, product quality or prices should be the easiest dimensions in which the individual firm can make adjustments. Changes in market scope or the degree of customization, on the other hand, are a more long-term matter and not all that easy to carry out in the electrotechnical industry. Although mobility barriers must be considered in each specific case, market scope and customization generally determine the main barriers.

Since the penetration of a widespread market is a resource demanding affair, distributors often play a dominant role. Hence, control of marketing channels is frequently a decisive mobility barrier to strategic groups operating on such markets. Another example of mobility barriers is the kind of intense, long-term customer relations that bring advantages to strategic groups characterized by a high level of individually adapted products.

In the strategic states model, the market scope of a company is specified by a 'number of segments that are being penetrated' (i.e. segment penetration), while customization is an operationalization of segment adaptation. Thus, a conclusion from the discussion above is that the strategic states model is appropriate even for the classification of competitors and identification of strategic groups. Hence, a company or any other organizational unit has the possibility to group competitors, search for a defendable position and develop its own business strategy following the strategic states model.

In the following I will describe strategic groups in the electrotechnical industry, and specifically manufacturers of industrial robots on the global market (Pehrsson 1990 and 1991 present other examples). As market scope and customization determine important mobility barriers in the industry, the dimensions in the strategic states model will be emphasized in the grouping of competitors.

Industrial robot manufacturers in general produce automation systems composed of robots, computerized control systems, tools and other complementary equipment as well as providing know-how about robot applications. There are six major applications: assembly, material handling/machine loading, painting, spot welding, arc welding and machining. A small number of applications represents a narrow system, while a larger number represents a broader system. This means that manufacturers offering broad systems are better able to adapt their products to the specific needs of a variety of individual customers.

The automotive industry is one major segment of the market, the electronics industry another. Other segments consist of customers requiring small volumes and quick deliveries, and so on.

From my analysis of secondary data from 1986 (Dataquest 1987) four distinct strategic groups of manufacturers emerge on the global industrial robot market (Figure 2.5). The 15 companies altogether accounted for 70 per cent of the revenues on the market, which in 1986 were around SEK12 billion. Some of the companies specialize in robot manufacturing, while some are also engaged in other activities.

The dominant group consists of the world's largest robot companies, ASEA of Sweden and GMF. This is a coalition between General Motors and Fanuc of Japan.

The two groups of challengers had minor market shares and were composed of companies in varying degrees penetrating many segments and offering broad systems. Fanuc, Hitachi, Kawasaki, Nachi-Fuji, Toshiba and Yaskawa are Japanese companies, while Cincinatti and Unimation are US based. Kuka is based in Germany. All these challengers probably have the ambition to become dominants, but this will require far higher market shares.

Nichers (Graco, Adept, Cloos, Matsushita and others) specialize in a few applications, such as painting or assembly and penetrate limited market segments. In particular, Matsushita of Japan has succeeded and in 1986 accounted for a 6 per cent share of the total market.

As in many other markets, the large dominants and the small nichers

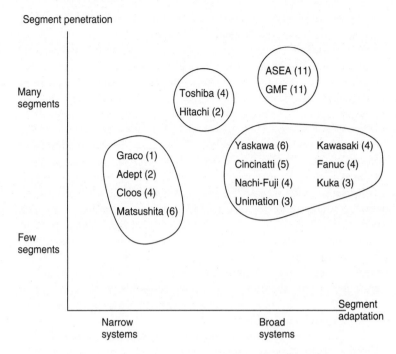

Figure 2.5 Strategic groups of manufacturers on the global market for industrial robots (market shares by revenues in 1986 in parentheses)

on the global market presumably have the most favourable basis for survival. In the case of the dominants, large volumes facilitate economies of scale and low costs, which protect these companies from the threat of price cuts. The nichers are able to survive and have decent lives by becoming experts in narrow systems or few segments.

The two strategic groups that might be referred to as challengers can choose between different business strategies for the future. Either they can try to make an impact on the market as a whole and then perhaps become members of the dominant group, or they can try to find niches or, of course, they could try to create new paths.

STRATEGIC STATES AND PERFORMANCE: A STUDY OF SWEDISH COMPANIES IN GERMANY

Since every business has to be financially defensible in the long term, it is important to be aware of general relationships between business strategies and companies' performance. In order to facilitate the formulation of business strategies in a given market it may therefore be helpful to examine the strategies of profitable companies.

Various universal models can be found in the strategic management literature prescribing, for example, high profitability for cost leaders and companies that follow the focus strategy (Porter 1980). Other models rely on research that searches for relationships contained in broad categories, such as industrial and consumer goods companies (e.g. Galbraith and Schendel 1983; Rumelt 1982). Samiee and Roth (1992) espouse this tradition, comparing performance levels of companies offering standardized products with those offering less standardized products in a wide range of industries.

However, there is a lack of studies concerning the relationship between strategy and performance in one particular industry and such studies should therefore be carried out. More specifically, we need to know more about the strategies employed by high-performing companies as compared with those of low-performing companies. The main reason for suggesting a focus on a single industry is that generalizations across dispersed industries obviously imply problems in defining and measuring strategy and performance due to the varying premises applying in different industries.

This leads to the exploratory question posed by the study (Pehrsson 1995a) presented in this section of the chapter: Is it possible to identify any strategic state at a certain point in time that is more profitable than another state in the electrotechnical industry? The empirical study deals with German subsidiaries of Swedish companies manufacturing electrotechnical products, and tries to identify the strategic states of high and low performers. Performance at a specific point in time is measured by financial performance as compared to the company's expectations. Germany is considered as an extensive, highly competitive market for international companies and this would mean that gaining awareness of profitable business strategies employed in that country is of crucial importance.

The empirical study suggests that one must carefully consider the advantages to be gained by penetration of just a few selected segments of the German market. A concentration strategy such as this demands a thorough market investigation that would take into account the whole of the German market and then distinguish specific segments.

Another normative conclusion is that a relatively high share of the invoicing should concern customized products and services, following an adaptation strategy. In order to balance off the relatively risky but potentially more profitable customized orders, one may consider offering a certain amount of pure standardized products. In this question of priorities, access to information about customer preferences is necessary. Considerable variation in preferences will require perhaps that a local product development function must be established.

A final normative conclusion is that the financial objectives regarding German subsidiaries have to be realistically formulated. One has to be conscious of the need for financial persistence and that there are no guarantees that an increase in volume will lead to higher profitability.

Identification of profitable strategic states

In order to search for the relationship between strategic states and financial performance, and to be able to compare the high-performing and the low-performing companies, the empirical study used quantitative cross-sectional data. The data concern strategic states and financial performance of West German subsidiaries of Swedish companies manufacturing electrotechnical products.

The strategic states model is operationalized into six variables, where four represent segment penetration and two apply to the degree of segment adaptation. Based on these independent variables, six hypotheses comparing the strategic states of high-performing and low-performing companies have been formulated.

The test of the hypotheses shows statistically significant differences between high- and low-performing companies when it comes to the share of the three largest orders in the invoicing and the share of the invoicing for customized orders.

Sample and data collection

The sample comprises all the 66 Swedish subsidiaries (Jahrbuch 1989) in West Germany that were engaged in the electrotechnical industry in 1989. The reason for focusing on Swedish firms only is twofold. As these companies are generally open, it is possible to capture information for research purposes. Furthermore, an investigation of companies of a single country of origin implies that management values can be expected to be relatively homogeneous.

Germany is a very important market for Swedish companies. This, together with the severe competition on that market, makes it of crucial importance for companies to be aware of business strategies and their effects. Additionally, companies in this country present an interesting study sample.

Mail questionnaires were used in the data collection process. The questionnaires were answered by the companies' presidents with 37 questionnaires filled in and returned, giving a 56 per cent response rate. As always, it was difficult to determine why certain companies failed to answer the questionnaire but the following causes have been identified: four companies never filled in questionnaires; three companies were no longer Swedish subsidiaries; two companies had divested their activities in West Germany; one had only recently established itself on the market.

The median turnover in 1988 was SEK40 million, with the largest accounting for SEK525 million and the smallest for SEK3.5 million. The companies were marketing products such as devices for direct current, electronic measuring instruments, power electronics, heating technology, telecommunications technology, computerized process control, industrial robots and transformers.

Variables and hypotheses

The two dimensions that specify strategic states are operationalized by using six variables. Four are used for the penetration of market segments and the other two concern the degree of adaptation.

Segment penetration is referred to in the study as the degree of customer dependence. The term customer here means users and not intermediaries, although the latter also have to be frequently approached in marketing. Thus, the degree of customer dependence in 1988 was measured by the number of customers and customer structure in terms of the three largest customers' share of the invoicing. A large share means that a small number of customers dominate, while a small share corresponds to a more uniform customer distribution. Since individual customers often place orders more than once a year, the study also considers the number of orders and the three largest orders' share of the invoicing.

The degree of segment adaptation in 1988 was measured by the average period of time from order booking to final invoicing. Extensive customer adaptation obviously requires long project times. But since adapted products can be combined with more standardized products, the share of the invoicing for customized orders was measured as well.

Although the median return on the capital employed was 4 per cent in 1988 for those companies that were able to specify this parameter in the questionnaire, there are a number of difficulties in interpreting financial measures, such as return on capital employed. Frequently, different companies define such measures in different ways. Furthermore, transactions within company groups constitute a source of uncertainty as regards estimations of the extent to which the performance of a single company should be regarded as 'real' performance.

Accordingly, it was found more appropriate in this study to consider financial performance in relation to company expectations. Subsidiaries that showed good or very good financial performance in 1988, when compared with their expectations, are referred to as high performers, whereas those with poor or acceptable performance are called low performers.

The quantitative questions in the questionnaire were complemented with open-ended questions to facilitate interpretation of the data. These questions concerned year of the company's establishment in West Germany, turnover, organizational responsibilities, products and customer types catered for.

Despite the fact that the questionnaire had been pretested on several occasions, it was accompanied by a letter of introduction explaining the important concepts. In order to facilitate the interpretation of the information generated in the study, I interviewed two respondents in the sample and held a number of seminars attended by both practitioners and academicians.

It was assumed that concentrated penetration of only a few selected market segments or customers was of vital importance in the electro-technical industry, where the number of competitors is large. If we compare high and low performers, we arrive at the first hypothesis:

Hypothesis 1: High-performing companies have fewer customers than low-performing companies.

In marketing, focus on a limited number of customers implies that resources can be utilized effectively. Even though a relatively strong dependence on few customers might lead to potentially weaker bargaining power, the second hypothesis has the following meaning:

Hypothesis 2: The three largest customers account for a larger share of the invoicing in high-performing companies compared with that of low-performing companies.

A parallel discussion concerning order booking gives the third and fourth hypotheses:

Hypothesis 3: High-performing companies book fewer orders than low-performing companies.

Hypothesis 4: The three largest orders account for a larger share of the invoicing in high-performing companies compared with that of low-performing companies.

Each company has to balance customer adaptation against standardization of its offer. Adaptation to customer requirements implies that competitive measures other than price become important. Adaptation frequently embraces the possibility of customer loyalties and barriers to competition. On the other hand, extensive adaptation to individual needs can be very risky, as the company's flexibility will be restricted. Standardization of products often means a possibility of generating stable liquidity, even though customers can then more easily compare alternative offers.

Following the assumption that in the electrotechnical industry customized orders will lead to better results than standardized products, we arrive at the two final hypotheses:

Hypothesis 5: The average time between order booking and final invoicing is longer for high-performing companies than low-performing companies.

Hypothesis 6: Customized orders account for a larger share of the invoicing in high-performing companies compared with that of low-performing companies.

Test of hypotheses

Table 2.2 shows the data for high performers and low performers on the six variables. Nineteen companies stated that, compared with their expectations for 1988, their financial performance was poor or just acceptable. These companies are called 'low performers'. Those eighteen companies that showed good or very good results in the same respect are called 'high performers'.

Chi-square tests showed two statistically significant differences at the 95 per cent confidence level. The fourth and sixth hypotheses are therefore accepted and the others are rejected. This means that two kinds of relationships between strategic states and performance apply to the study sample:

The three largest orders account for a larger share of the invoicing in high-performing companies compared with that of low-performing companies.

Table 2.2 Data concerning segment penetration and segment adaptation for West German subsidiaries of Swedish electrotechnical companies, 1988

Independent variables	Low performers[1] (n=19)	High performers[2] (n=18)
Segment penetration		
No. of customers	median=300	median=300
The three largest customers' share of the invoicing	mean=26%	mean=32%
No. of orders	median=2.000	median=2.000
The three largest orders' share of the invoicing (*)	mean=16%	mean=26%
Segment adaptation		
No. of days from order to final invoicing on average	median=60	median=30
Share of the invoicing for customer orders (*)	mean=44%	mean=72%

Source: Pehrsson 1995a (reprinted by permission of John Wiley & Sons Ltd)
Notes:
* Statistically significant difference at P< 0.05
1 Poor or acceptable financial performance compared with company expectations
2 Good or very good financial performance compared with company expectations

> Customized orders account for a larger share of the invoicing in high-performing companies compared with that of low-performing companies.

Characteristics of high and low performers

The data analysis shows that the strategic states of the two company groups are significantly different as regards two independent variables. The three largest orders' share of the invoicing in those eighteen companies that can be called high performers accounted for a higher value in comparison with that of the nineteen low performers. The mean values are 26 per cent and 16 per cent respectively (Figure 2.6). Moreover, customized orders accounted for a larger share of the invoicing for the high performance companies compared to the share of low performers. In this case the mean values are 72 per cent and 44 per cent respectively.

Products offered by high-performing companies include systems for computerized control of industrial processes, technical equipment for

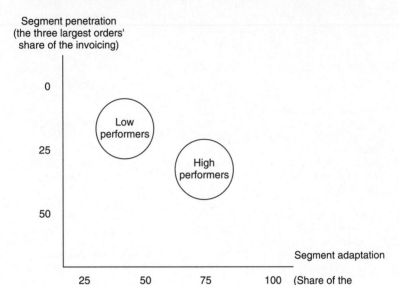

Figure 2.6 Strategic states of West German subsidiaries of Swedish electrotechnical companies, 1988
Source: Pehrsson 1995a (reprinted by permission of John Wiley & Sons Ltd)

large ships, industrial robots and computerized machines for manufacturing. Low performers offer products such as lamps, measurement instruments, washing machines, electric tools and office equipment.

The median high performance company was established in the western part of Germany in 1974, and the median low performance company in 1980. When it comes to turnover in 1988, the median values were DM9 million and DM13 million respectively.

Thus, knowledge of the German market seems to be a reasonable explanation of success. As it takes time to develop a competitive business strategy in a market, experience is needed to find a defendable strategic state. Experience is particularly important for learning how the major competitors in the market behave.

Another possible explanation of the good results achieved by the high performers could be frequent use of local functions for product development and adaptation to local premises. Some 40 per cent of the high performance category reported local responsibility and responsiveness in this respect (Table 2.3). This market sensitivity was not shown by low performers. For this company category, only 20 per cent

Table 2.3 Local responsibilities of West German subsidiaries of Swedish electrotechnical companies, 1988

Local responsibilities	No. of companies	
	Low performers (n=19)	High performers (n=18)
Product development	4	7
Design[1]	4	7
Manufacturing	10	6
Sales[2]	18	18
Service[3]	4	3

Source: Pehrsson 1995a (reprinted by permission of John Wiley & Sons Ltd)
Notes:
1 Including 'software design' (2 companies)
2 Including 'marketing' (1) and 'projecting' (1)
3 Including 'installation' (1)

of the companies reported local responsiveness as regards product development.

Furthermore, only one-third of the high performers manufactured their goods in the former West Germany. In many cases, manufacturing would have been done instead by the parent companies in Sweden. No matter whether manufacturing was localized in Sweden or elsewhere, centralization of this function would have facilitated production planning and the exploitation of scale effects. Over half of the low performers reported the existence of local manufacturing.

The most successful subsidiaries in the study concentrated their marketing efforts on relatively few market segments. At the same time, these companies would to a large extent adapt their offers to suit the selected customers. This included customization and to a certain extent localization to fit local demands.

Concentration and adaptation enable a company to build up stable and long-term relations with its customers. As the process continues the customers will gradually find that the number of available alternative suppliers from which to choose decreases. Long-term relations imply loyalty and therefore create barriers against other established and potential competitors. Consequently, the pressure for low prices weakens and, as long as costs are tightly controlled, concentration and adaptation mean a promising strategic state as regards profitability.

However, high risks are involved in the strategic state defined by concentration and adaptation. First, problems with payment or other hardships which the customer must endure might eventually have serious consequences for the company. These would be caused by the dependence and the corresponding restrictions on freedom of action. Second, as the products are presumably adapted to very specific requirements, they cannot easily be available to customers in other market segments.

The most successful companies in the study have probably reached a balance between standardized 'inventory orders' and customized orders. Standardized products which can generally be delivered at a moment's notice will usually generate stable liquidity that can balance off the more hazardous and often more profitable customized orders. Furthermore, a certain degree of standardization enables the company to exploit the learning effect resulting from the recurrence of the activities connected with its organizational functions. This in turn makes it possible to reduce the company's marginal costs.

3

IMPORTANT CHOICES IN THE DEVELOPMENT OF INTERNATIONAL BUSINESS STRATEGIES

The study of strategic states and performance reported in the last section of Chapter 2 gave rise to a more thorough discussion about three important choices in the development of international business strategies: a business unit's choice between penetration of a few or a variety of market segments, between separate products or systems of products, and between product standardization or adaptation. The previous chapter briefly indicated the decision problems and some normative conclusions. In this chapter these important choices will be more completely discussed, still within the frame given by the strategic states model. The first three sections highlight identification of alternatives, while the final section concerns strategy evaluation.

The identification of strategic alternatives is generally the starting-point of the strategy choice process, and alternatives then need to be evaluated in the light of internal premises. Thus, the first section (pp. 39–52) discusses identification of market segments to choose from. This is followed by a discussion of the critical product concept definition, implying certain strategy problems as regards the offering of separate products compared to systems of products (pp. 53–9). The third section of the chapter (pp. 59–77) treats alternatives when it comes to international product standardization and adaptation. Finally, major ingredients in the strategy evaluation procedure are put forward (pp. 77–9).

PENETRATION OF A FEW OR A VARIETY OF MARKET SEGMENTS?

A business unit's choice between the penetration of relatively few or a variety of market segments will be considered in this section. The choice will be highlighted by a theoretical discussion of industrial market segmentation and exemplified by a specific case.

Industrial market segmentation in theory

Markets consist of buyers that differ in many ways. They can be distinguished by specific demands, resources, geographic localization, purchasing behaviour and attitudes towards the products they buy. These variables can be used in market segmentation, dividing the market into groups of buyers whose needs are essentially the same. The term 'needs' should be, however, interpreted in a wider context than just as product characteristics. Besides their needs of products, buyers differ in their need of, for example, information, delivery service or technical support. Additionally, buyers can be distinguished from one another by their willingness and ability to pay.

Many authors have discussed market segmentation (e.g. Abell and Hammond 1979; Bonoma and Shapiro 1983). It is a common view that effective segmentation divides a market into parts:

1 that are identifiable and also large enough when it comes to purchasing volume;
2 that are potentially profitable for companies penetrating a specific segment;
3 that are accessible to penetration;
4 that are defendable against competition.

The condition concerning the segment's size means simply that it must be possible to measure purchasing volumes in different segments.

It is an accepted view that the market segmentation procedure consists primarily of three steps:

1 Data collection: The data should have a cross-sectional character and be valid for a large sample of buyers. If the analyst is uncertain of the appropriate segmentation variables, he/she should first conduct a number of personal interviews with the representatives of the buyers concerned in order to understand their position. The analyst should then be able to specify the variables.
2 Data analysis: The data can be analysed in the simplest manner by using cross-tables between different variables. In this process, one searches for variables that indicate the most obvious groups of buyers.
3 Profilation: Each segment is relevantly described and assumes a certain character. The segments can be described either according to

the specific demands or requirements of the buyers, such as price sensitivity and other attitudes, or according to the buyers' identity in terms of, for instance, their geographic localization.

As markets are constantly changing and developing, the market segmentation procedure must be repeated regularly. Companies that initiate the segmentation themselves will be a part of the driving force and will therefore have a good opportunity of anticipating the development. Companies that only react to changes will most probably find that they are controlled by external events.

Industrial markets can be basically segmented by the use of many of the same variables that are employed in consumer market segmentation, such as geography, benefits sought and usage rate. Yet other variables may be also employed. Bonoma and Shapiro (1983) propose a classification of segmentation variables for industrial markets in which demographic variables are the most important ones. These are followed by the operating variables, down to the personal characteristics of the individual buyer.

Demographic variables

- Industry – which industries that buy our product should we focus on?
- Company size – what size of companies should we focus on?
- Location – what geographical areas should we focus on?

Operating variables

- Technology – what customer technologies should we focus on?
- User/non-user status – should we focus on heavy, medium, light users or non-users?
- Customer capabilities – should we focus on customers needing many services or few services?

Purchasing variables

- Organization of the purchasing function – should we focus on companies with highly centralized or decentralized purchasing organizations?
- Power structure – should we focus on companies which are engineering dominated, financially dominated, etc.?
- Nature of existing relationship – should we focus on companies with which we have strongly established relationships or should we go after the more desirable companies?

- General purchase policies – should we focus on companies which prefer leasing, service contracts, systems purchases, sealed bidding?
- Purchasing criteria – should we focus on companies who seek quality, service, price?

Situational variables

- Urgency – should we focus on companies that need quick and sudden deliveries or services?
- Specific application – should we focus on certain chosen applications of our product, rather than on all applications?
- Size of order – should we focus on large or small orders?

Personal characteristics

- Buyer–seller similarity – should we focus on companies whose people and values are similar to ours?
- Attitudes toward risk – should we focus on risk-taking or risk-avoiding customers?
- Loyalty – should we focus on companies that show high loyalty to their suppliers?

These are the major questions that industrial marketers should ask themselves when determining which segments and customers to serve. By choosing segments rather than the whole market, the business unit can deliver more real value than its competitors and charge a premium for it.

Within a chosen target industry, a business can further segment by customer size, where separate programmes for dealing with large and small customers can be set up. For instance, major accounts could be handled by the unit itself, whereas smaller accounts could be processed in cooperation with the distributors. Furthermore, within a certain target industry and customer size, the business can segment by purchase criteria, for example.

In evaluating different market segments and deciding on the number of segments that should be penetrated, one needs to look at the four segment conditions discussed above, and the objectives, as well as the business strategy of the unit itself.

A potential segment should have an appropriate size and growth characteristics. Here, the company has to make an evaluation of both the segments with large sales volumes that require heavy resources, as well as of the small segments. In evaluating segment growth, it is important to be aware of competitors' interest in growing segments, and that some competitors might try to enter those and depress their profitability.

A segment with a desirable size may still not be attractive from the point of view of profitability. In determining the profitability attractiveness of a market or a market segment, the business needs to appraise the impact that rivalry among the established competitors may have on profitability and assess the bargaining power of the buyers and the suppliers, as well as the danger of substitutes and potential entrants (Porter 1980).

Even if a segment has positive size, is attractive from the profitability point of view, is not surrounded by too high barriers of entry and is defendable, the business unit needs to consider its own objectives and business strategy in relation to that segment. Even if the segment fits the objectives, the business still has to consider whether it possesses sufficient skills and resources in order to succeed in that segment.

By evaluation of different segments the business hopes to find one or more market segments worth entering. One must decide which and how many segments to serve. When selecting more than one segment to serve, Kotler (1991; 284) stresses that the business unit should pay close attention to segment interrelationships as regards costs, performance, and technology. A unit that carries a fixed cost has perhaps the possibility of adding products to absorb and share some of the costs.

Furthermore, the choice of market segments to penetrate implies a consideration of which business strategy to follow: divergence or concentration. In this assessment of strategies, a number of trade-offs are to be made and the implications of factors such as the following have to be interpreted. Factors that might favour divergence include:

- low volumes in single market segments;
- low growth rate in single market segments;
- non-repeat purchases of the product in question;
- unstable and changing market conditions;
- many similar market segments;
- low market costs for additional market segments.

Factors that might favour concentration include:

- high volumes in single market segments;
- high growth rate in single market segments;
- repeat purchase of the product in question;
- stable market conditions;
- few comparable market segments;
- high marketing costs for additional market segments.

The discussed segmentation procedure can be classified as a 'contractible method' (Albaum *et al.* 1989), which involves a systematic screening of possible market segments and leads to elimination of the less promising and further investigation of the more interesting ones. The major criteria in this process are the four segment conditions (identifiability and size, profitability, accessibility and defendability), and the objectives and the business strategy of the business unit in question.

An 'expansive' approach to market segmentation (still according to Albaum *et al.*) takes the home market or the existing market core as its starting-point. Market selection over time is based upon similarities between segments so that one expands from one segment to the next, introducing a minimum of changes. This is a type of experience-based market selection procedure, often referred to as the 'next neighbour' approach. Here, it is presupposed that a business unit has one single market that might be treated as the base market segment. This is selected either because it represents the unit's strongest marketing centre or because it is intended to turn into the focal point.

Segmenting the industrial robot market in Western Europe: the Robotics case

What kinds of segments exist within the market for industrial robots in Western Europe? One group of the early users of industrial robots were car manufacturers. But are there any other segments which can be distinguished?

Robotics AB is a fictive Swedish company that manufactures and offers industrial robots. Sales companies have been established in Scandinavia (Sweden and Norway), while in Central Europe Robotics employs agents (England, France and Germany). Hitherto, no representation has been set up in Southern Europe (Italy and Spain).

Robotics is familiar of course with the segment of car manufacturers, which has been well penetrated and delivered to for a long time. As this segment seemed to have been getting increasingly mature, the company required information about the number of segments of the industrial robot market in Western Europe. For this reason a market analyst was engaged.

The case (more thoroughly reported on in Pehrsson 1991) continues with a presentation of the industrial robot system. After that the situation of the using companies is briefly described, together with the market development. The major part of the case deals with the study of the market analyst. First, the data collection method is described.

Second, the variables in the mail questionnaire are presented. The analysis of the data and the identification of the segments follows.

What is an industrial robot?

Figure 3.1 illustrates the components of the industrial robot system. The control system, including the terminal, corresponds to the human brain and its nerves. The working machine resembles the human skeleton and muscles, and the clutching-tongs represent hands and fingers. If a detector is present, this constitutes the eyes of the robot.

The control system decides in what order, how fast and how much the elements of the robot will move. The pattern of the movements is designed by an operator who applies computer programs at the terminal.

The working machine moves the clutching-tongs. The movements are made possible by electric, hydraulic or pneumatic energy. In order to move and manipulate an object, at least six degrees of freedom are required.

Optical or mechanical detectors enable the robot continually to program itself. For instance, it can distinguish and seize a particular object from the conveyor belt.

Robots for industrial applications are divided according to their application areas. Process robots handle tools, such as welding electrodes, mouthpieces for painting or polishing discs. Welding, painting and assembly are major applications of process robots. Robots for material handling move materials, components or products from place to place, another major application.

The situation of the using companies

Installation of a robot implies varying costs for the using company. There are two factors that primarily decide the cost level: the type of robot and the accompanying system, and the degree of changes necessary in order to adapt the entire production environment to automation. In a survey study, conducted by a Swedish industrial association (Sveriges Mekanförbund), of the first 500 Swedish industrial robot installations, only 20 per cent of the using companies referred to financial reasons as the main investment motive (*Modern Produktion* 1986b). According to this study, environmental reasons and the need to acquire technological experience were the dominant motives.

An industrial robot is most suitable and profitable for the production

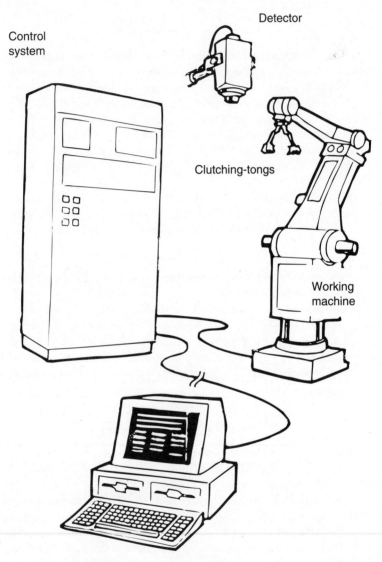

Control
system

Detector

Clutching-tongs

Working
machine

Figure 3.1 Components of an industrial robot system

of middle-sized series. When dealing with series covering more than one million pieces, however, it is normally more profitable for the using company to invest in stationary automatic systems, for example transfer machines. Manual machine operations are generally most profitable in short production series.

What are the important factors to note if a company is going to automate a section of its workshop and install industrial robots?

Primarily, it is important for a user to think in terms of systems. No basic problems will be solved if one simply puts an industrial robot on the floor. Then it will not be used and only cost money. We also stress the importance of giving practically involved personnel the opportunity to influence the production environment.

A major reason for bad installations is a belief that a robot can solve all production problems. This is a typical argument: 'As we have bought an expensive robot it will be used to carry out the most difficult procedure in our factory.' That company will be disappointed when it discovers that nothing works. It is necessary to turn the argument around and say that, even though the robot is expensive, we have to start with the simplest application in the factory. This is crucial as automatic production systems are very complex.

(Chairman of The Swedish Industrial Robot Association,
Modern Produktion 1986a)

Development of the market

Even though the use of industrial robots has increased in a number of countries, the total market growth decreased around 1985. Many experts believed that the prior fast growth of the market would never occur again. To a large extent this was caused by the fact that a dominant part of the automotive industry had obviously invested in basic robot systems.

Dataquest is a company that compiles statistics for the industrial robot market. The value of the world market for industrial robots showed a 12 per cent decrease in 1987 as compared to 1986 (Dataquest 1987). The automotive industry accounted for the largest decline (−21 per cent). When it comes to applications, welding and painting showed the clearest decrease between 1987 and 1986. The value of the West European market (Belgium, England, France, Italy, Scandinavia, Spain, Germany) declined by approximately 6 per cent.

Table 3.1 presents turnover and market shares in terms of the turnover for the largest manufacturers that were delivering to Western Europe in 1986. It also shows the number of delivered industrial robots.

The yearly volume of industrial robots delivered on the Swedish market increased during the period as can be seen from Table 3.2.

The analyst's collection of the market data

In order to accomplish his task, the market analyst compiled a database containing information about a large number of companies that were real or potential users of industrial robots. The size of the companies varied but all belong to the manufacturing industries of metal goods, machines and electrotechnical products. The companies are located in Scandinavia (Sweden, Norway), Central Europe (England, France, Germany), and Southern Europe (Italy, Spain).

In this systematic study, the analyst first held five personal interviews with the representatives of randomly chosen companies using industrial robots in their production. These interviews were necessary to enable the focusing on the variables relevant to the study. The analyst also found that production managers have in general the best knowledge of their companies' use of industrial robots.

Table 3.1 Turnover, market shares and number of delivered industrial robots for manufacturers, 1986

Companies	Turnover (US$ million)	Share of industry turnover %	No. of delivered industrial robots
ASEA	114	29	1,255
Cloos	58	15	248
GMF	37	10	299
KUKA	26	6	296
Unimation	14	4	117
Yaskawa	11	3	222
DeVilbiss	9	2	93
Fanuc	9	2	223
Nachi-Fujikoshi	9	2	159
Toshiba	9	2	51
Others	94	25	1162
Total	US$390 million	100 %	4,125 robots

Source: Dataquest, 1987

Table 3.2 Number of delivered industrial robots to Swedish industry

	1983	1984	1985	1986	Until 1986
Applications					
Material handling	71	87	83	126	960
Welding	56	102	97	124	798
Assembly	4	11	59	46	124
Other applications	48	93	62	41	501
Total	179	293	301	337	2,383
Using manufacturing industries					
Metal goods	28	64	93	46	332
Machines	39	81	67	94	854
Electrotechnical products	11	12	38	43	198
Vehicles	60	97	64	119	706
Other manufacturing	41	39	39	35	293
Total	179	293	301	337	2,383

Source: The Swedish Industrial Robot Association, March 1987

A telephone survey followed the personal interviews. The analyst established personal contact with the production managers of sixty Western European companies in the manufacturing industries of metal goods, machines and electrotechnical products. (During the interviews he had a feeling that these industries knew many companies that were interested in industrial robots.) Fifty production managers finally agreed to reply to a number of questions, and the analyst was then able to compile his database.

Variables used in the questionnaire

The analyst decided to use five variables to describe the companies' use of industrial robots. The first variable indicates the serial number of each company in the survey.

The next three variables describe the demographic premises of the companies. Each company in the database thus belongs to one of the three manufacturing industries of metal goods, machines and electrotechnical products. Furthermore, the headquarters of the companies are located in Scandinavia, Central Europe or Southern Europe. The third demographic variable refers to the size of the companies, in terms of the turnover in 1987. The analyst found that the companies could be divided into three distinct groups: 50–500, 500–1,000 and more than 1,000 million SEK in turnover for 1987.

One variable describes the companies' production activities. Each company was here asked to specify the average length of its manufacturing series. When the analyst classified the information regarding the length of the series, the companies were divided into three groups: less than 500 pieces, between 500 and 2,000 pieces, and more than 2,000 pieces.

Table 3.3 shows the variables used in the questionnaire, the possible values and the contents of the values.

Segment identification

The general demands on a market segment imply that the segment must be large enough to make the marketing profitable. The segment must also be accessible to adapted marketing activities and defendable against competition.

Thus, the first step in the segmentation performed by the analyst was to figure out the way in which the market and its segments were to be measured. This facilitates the classification of companies into specific segments and makes it possible to apply the classification to a company which has not even participated in the particular study.

As discussed earlier, industrial robots are normally most suitable for manufacturing of middle-sized series. When it comes to the companies in the study, only those which manufactured more than 2,000 pieces on average in 1987 were attractive to automation using industrial robots. However, there is a risk that very long series motivating stationary automatic systems may be found among these companies. Table 3.4 shows that 31 companies fulfil this requirement.

As the previous analysis shows, the only promising companies in connection with automation are those who manufacture series covering more than 2,000 pieces and a potential classification problem emerges. In order for a company which has not participated in the referred study is to be classified, then primary information about the length of the manufacturing series would be necessary. The importance of the access to such information could, however, be diminished in cases when there is a high correlation between series and, for instance, turnover. Information about turnover is available from public company registers.

Table 3.4 presents a cross-tabulation between the variables of series and turnover. Twenty-five of the thirty-one companies that in 1987 manufactured series covering more than 2,000 pieces on average

Table 3.3 Variables describing companies' need of industrial robots

Variable	Possible values	Content of the values
Number	1–50	Serial number of each company
Industry	1, 2, 3	Main manufacturing in 1987: 1 = manufacturing of metal goods 2 = manufacturing of machines 3 = manufacturing of electrotechnical products
Geography	1, 2, 3	Headquarters location in 1987: 1 = Scandinavia (Sweden or Norway) 2 = Central Europe (England, France or West Germany) 3 = Southern Europe (Italy or Spain)
Turnover	1, 2, 3	Turnover in 1987: 1 = SEK 50–500 million 2 = SEK 500–1,000 million 3 = more than SEK 1,000 million
Series	1, 2, 3	Average length of manufacturing series in 1987: 1 = less than 500 pieces 2 = 500–2,000 pieces 3 = more than 2,000 pieces

Source: Pehrsson 1991

Table 3.4 Distribution of the companies studied regarding average length of manufacturing series and turnover, 1987

Turnover (SEK millions in 1987)	Series (Average no. of pieces in manufacturing series in 1987)		
	less than 500	500–2,000	More than 2,000
50–500	3	3	3
500–1,000	3	3	3
more than 1,000	3	4	25

Source: Pehrsson, 1991

accounted the same year for a turnover of more than SEK 1,000 million. Based on the study of the analyst, it is a good approximation to represent manufacturing companies with long series by manufacturing companies with a high turnover.

51

Hitherto, one Western European segment for industrial robots has been identified: manufacturing companies accounting for more than SEK 1,000 million. What pattern emerges when turnover and industry are cross-tabulated?

Table 3.5 clearly shows that the largest group consists of those twenty-six companies that reported more than SEK 1,000 million turnover in 1987 and which primarily manufacture metal goods such as bicycles and metal components for cars and refrigerators. Thus, the number of large companies manufacturing metal goods is sufficient in order to form a market segment. The large companies of the other industries seem to be too few in number to form separate segments. These companies could, however, be treated as one single segment.

Is it possible to identify further segments within 'metal goods manufacturers with more than SEK 1,000 million in a yearly turnover'? For instance, what is the geographical distribution of these twenty-six segments? Table 3.6 indicates that the segments are equally distributed

Table 3.5 Distribution of the companies studied regarding their turnover and main manufacturing, 1987

Turnover (SEK millions in 1987)	Industry (Main manufacturing in 1987)		
	Metal goods	Machines	Electrotechnical products
50–500	0	0	9
500–1,000	0	6	3
More than 1,000	26	6	0

Source: Pehrsson, 1991

Table 3.6 Distribution of the companies studied regarding industry and geographical location

Geography (Headquarters location in 1987)	Industry (Main manufacturing in 1987)		
	Metal goods	Machines	Electrotechnical products
Scandinavia (Sweden or Norway)	8	5	4
Central Europe (England, France or West Germany)	8	1	6
Southern Europe (Italy or Spain)	10	6	2

Source: Pehrsson, 1991

among the different geographical regions. As the companies are relatively numerous in Scandinavia, Central and Southern Europe, they should be treated in the regions as representatives of the three segments.

Adaptation possibilities for the marketing of industrial robots vary between Scandinavia, Central Europe and Southern Europe. The prices will probably have to be adapted depending on the competition. As regards penetration of potential customers using different communication techniques, attention must be paid to parameters such as language and culture. Such factors imply that the market ought to be segmented according to the geographical location of its potential customers.

Consequently, the West European market for industrial robots, excluding the car industry, can be divided into four segments, where all companies have a turnover of more than SEK 1,000 million (in parentheses: the number of companies in the study). These four segments are:

1 Companies that manufacture metal goods in Scandinavia (8).
2 Companies that manufacture metal goods in Central Europe (8).
3 Companies that manufacture metal goods in Southern Europe (10).
4 Companies that manufacture machines or electrotechnical products (6).

SEPARATE PRODUCTS OR SYSTEMS OF PRODUCTS?

The choice of a product concept for a company or business unit on an international market is not an easy task. For instance, which breadth of a product range is most appropriate? Should separate products or systems of products be pursued? As it is difficult to realize the implications of a product definition in advance, uncertainty plays an important role in the choice process. A choice of any strategic alternative could bring risks and a restriction of the freedom of action in implementing intentions. Thus, varying degrees of problems appear in the choice of product concept.

One can argue that the degree of problems in choices of product concepts is unique for every company and generalized patterns can hardly be found (Andrews 1971; Hatten *et al.* 1978). Such arguments primarily rely on in-depth studies in strategy research. On the other hand, the literature on industry competition (e.g. Porter 1980; Sölvell *et al.* 1991) advocates that strategic alternatives and the freedom of actions for companies are mainly formed and also restricted by the competitive environment in an industry. The basic framework for this literature implies that the problems noticed by companies in the course of choosing product concepts varies among industries.

In the contingency approach to business strategy (Galbraith and Schendel 1983; Ginsberg and Venkatraman 1985, and others) one states that a business strategy and correlated choice problems are contingent not only on the environmental situation, but also on the character of the company itself. This means that in principle a company of one character perceives problems in strategy choices differently from another company of different character. Such comparisons demand cross-sectional or similar methodologies that are suitable for comparative studies.

The purpose of the exploratory empirical study presented in Pehrsson (1993) is to compare the degrees of problems in strategy choices that are noticed by companies which mainly offer separate products, with corresponding perceptions of companies which mainly offer systems of products. The assumption is that a disparity exists. If this is correct, then a hypothetical difference helps us in trying to understand strategy choice problems for the two company categories.

In reviewing empirical research that applied contingency approaches, Ginsberg and Venkatraman (1985) found that organizational structure, leadership style, production technology and perceived need for organizational changes have been the most common ways to discriminate company characters. Hambrick and Lei (1985) emphasize that a company's character can also be denoted by market share, vertical integration and brand image.

Hill (1988) stresses that a company's ability to choose its business strategy is to a large extent a function of the characteristics of separate products. Any product can be viewed as a bundle of different characteristics. These can be varied in quantity and/or combined in different ways for a product. Relatively homogeneous products have few characteristics, while more complex products contain many characteristics.

However, differences in strategy problems between companies offering separate products and systems of products have been underestimated in previous empirical research. One fundamental distinction of a company's character is the way in which customers must be treated in the formulation of strategic alternatives. Separate products imply more bargaining power for customers as theoretically they have a better possibility to evaluate and compare more than one offer. Separate products also mean that strategic alternatives that involve distributors are more likely to be chosen.

Companies offering systems of products have to define these systems carefully. Which products are to be included and how are they related to each other? To what extent is it appropriate to combine physical products and immaterial services? Which characteristics of the system ought to be pursued? These questions entail, for instance, intricate choices of target customers, price and market promotion.

To facilitate empirical research, the products of the referred study were limited to metal goods, machines and electrotechnical products. In principle, the products are manufactured by the companies in the study or by other companies in the same groups.

The businesses of metal goods, machines and electrotechnical products have many similarities. Qualified engineering is normally a prerequisite, as well as production and marketing know-how. Although numerous subindustries exist, 'product' companies and 'system' companies in the focused industries are probably homogeneous enough in order to compare degrees of problems in strategy choices.

The framework for the study is based on a discussion of the components of business strategy and problems in strategy choices. Using a quantitative methodological approach,[1] the study then investigates Swedish companies that offer metal goods, machines and electro-technical products in Germany. All companies report to Swedish parent firms and are responsible for sales on the market. Some of the subsidiaries also take care of local manufacturing, design, etc.

Applying multivariate analyses, differences between the company characters are scrutinized. Where significant differences appear, strategy choice problems of companies mainly offering separate products and systems are discussed. Strategy choices of ABB Robotics and Ericsson Business Communications illustrate inherent problems.

The empirical findings of the referred study of Swedish subsidiaries in Germany support a hypothetical difference between company categories with regard to perceptions of problems in choices of business strategies. Companies that offer separate products demonstrate different perceptions compared with companies that offer systems of products. The hypothesis is valid for companies or groups that manufacture metal goods, machines and electrotechnical products and offer them for sale in a market.

Problems in choosing product qualities appear for both company categories. Yet, the signification of this varies. As a system consists of a number of products and services, the measurement and control of quality is more complex for 'system' companies compared with 'product' companies. The extent to which customization and standardization are to be applied is also a problematic choice in this context. If customization goes too far, then it is difficult to reach scale effects. On the other hand, pure standardization implies vulnerability to price competition.

The balance between customization of a system and standardization as an effort to reach reproducibility is a dominant problem for 'system' companies.

Product companies are generally more exposed to price competition, and choices of cost levels therefore represent a concern for this company category.

Components of business strategy

As the referred study is exploratory in nature, rather broad components of business strategy can be appropriately selected. Miller (1987), in reviewing the work of Hofer and Schendel (1978), Miles and Snow (1978), Henderson (1979), Porter (1980), Hambrick (1983), Dess and Davis (1984) and others, concluded that important components of business strategy discussed again and again were those of scope, differentiation and cost control. However, Miller argues that there is no way to prove, and we have no desire to claim, that these are in any way the only strategy components. Obviously, the interest generated by the studies cited indicates that these components or variants thereof have enjoyed much prominence.

Each component consists of a number of attributes or characteristics, which can be summed to give a representation of the degree to which a certain business strategy is pursued. Every characteristic, and of course the component itself, can be pursued to a greater or lesser extent. The components are not mutually exclusive. For instance, firms can be high on both scope and differentiation.

The scope component refers to the product/market scope that the business caters for and can be characterized as follows: the breadth of the product range, the variety of customer types, the number of customers and their geographical distribution. Most writers on strategy discuss this component. Chandler (1962) has been followed by Porter (1980) and others.

In high differentiation, one strives to create product customization and customer loyalty by uniquely meeting a particular customer need. Product appeal may be psychological in that advertising and prestige pricing are used to create a favourable image. Where the product is standardized in nature, it is probably perceived as a commodity. The choice by the buyer then is largely based on price and service, and pressure for intense price and service competition results.

Irrespective of the degrees of product customization and standardization, product quality can be pursued to a greater or lesser extent. Thus, the differentiation component can be characterized by the degree of product customization, the degree of product standardization, price levels and product quality.

The cost control component involves the extent to which the firm tightly controls costs in its business. Costs include manufacturing, design, advertising or other sales efforts. Cost levels characterize the cost control component of business strategy. Cost control and also pricing demand various financial calculations. To summarize, the components of business strategy that are characterized in the study are:

- scope (breadth of product range, variety of customer types, number of customers, customers' geographical distribution);
- differentiation (product customization, product standardization, product quality, price levels);
- cost control (cost levels).

As business strategies are hierarchical in nature (Lorange 1980) and frequently exist at different organizational levels, such as the corporate level, the business family level and the business element level, a number of strategies are normally present in a company. In a large company, a high-level strategy tends to be an aggregation of lower level strategies. More than one strategy can also be present in a specific organizational unit. This means that strategic managers in a company often have to consider a number of degrees of product customization, product standardization, product qualities, etc.

A contemporary choice of business strategy could be problematic for many reasons. For instance, too few alternatives could exist or there could be a lack of knowledge of available options. Moreover, the pressure for a quick decision could be overwhelming and the financial or other effects of the decision could be very difficult to foresee because of information shortage. Thus, the treatment of uncertainty plays an important role in strategy choice processes (Pehrsson 1990). Uncertainty is something which strategic managers have to deal with. In fact Thompson (1967) identified uncertainty as the fundamental problem to be tackled by top-level managers.

Strategy choice problems of companies mainly offering separate products

For the companies in the study that mainly offer separate products, problems in choosing product qualities are a dominant factor. In this context, attention must be paid to determining whether a high-level quality should be pursued for the entire product range, or for only parts of it. This includes an assessment of the value of a narrow or broad range of separate products. No matter which quality level is decided, quality must be compared with market standards and secured within the company.

ABB Robotics is an illustrative example regarding product quality choices of companies in this category. Computerized robots for industrial applications, such as assembly, material handling, painting, welding and machining, constitute the main products of this Swiss and Swedish company. Robots are manufactured in Sweden and adapted to the needs of local customers by subsidiaries in various countries. The automotive industry is the major market segment, which means that Germany is very important for ABB Robotics.

As the level of quality and technology of competing industrial robots in Germany is generally high and uniform, suppliers seek to complement standardized products with application knowledge. This requires deep understanding of customers' production processes and needs. If ABB Robotics goes too far in product customization, however, it will be difficult to reach long series in manufacturing and appurtenant effects of scale. At the same time, robot manufacturing could be less interesting and quality could deteriorate.

Difficulties in choosing cost levels are another problem factor for 'product' companies. One interpretation of this stems from the connections between costs, prices and profitability. A customer's comparison of different offers on the market is facilitated by the presence of relatively distinct core products and, consequently, prices play an important role in the evaluation by the customer. Thus, pricing is frequently a decisive competitive mean for a company offering single products, and the ability to choose cost levels is crucial in order to reach profitability objectives.

Another interpretation addresses the relation between fixed costs and the need for sales volume. If fixed costs are high, there is a pressure for large volumes and, particularly under price competition, prices perhaps must be low. ABB Robotics strives to be a leader in technology, which means very high costs for research and development and a need for large volumes. At the same time, marketing and service become of vital importance.

The third factor underlying variables in strategy choices of companies that mainly offer separate products focuses on problems in market segmentation. As the choice of customer types theoretically requires an assessment of competition in available market segments, the stiff competition in Germany presumably creates uncertainty for involved companies. Once the desired customer types have been selected, competition obstructs a company's desire to increase the number of customers. The automotive industry is the most important market segment for ABB Robotics. To balance this single industry dependence, other customer types are presumably searched for. No matter what the choice, competition must be considered and knowledge of unfamiliar customers' patterns of requirements must be built up.

Strategy choice problems of companies mainly offering systems of products

Problems in deciding product qualities is a dominant factor for 'system' companies, as well as for 'product' companies. The meaning of the factor differs, however, for the categories. As a system can be composed of a physical product, complementing products and auxiliary services, quality must be measured and controlled to fit all components in the system. Thus, the choice of product quality for a system becomes very complex. In particular, service quality is an intricate issue involving evaluations relative to expectations or competition.

The Swedish company Ericsson is a major international group in the telecommunications industry and offers advanced products and systems for stationary and mobile communications in public and private networks. System knowledge and customization are important elements in the group's strategy. Long-term customer relations are necessary for a system supplier and Ericsson normally strives for total system responsibility.

The Business Communications area offers computerized communication systems for organizations that need to transmit data and voice using an exchange. A sales company represents this business area in Germany. In particular, service has become a decisive competitive mean in the German market for communication systems. Siemens is the market leader and creates the level of standard in the market. Thus, German customers of Ericsson Business Communications often refer to Siemens and demand high-quality service and product customization.

By nature, a system installation requires a high degree of adaptation to the needs of a single customer. However, complete customization implies that it is almost impossible to reach scale effects in production and low costs. The balance between customization of a system and standardization in order to reach reproducibility is a main problem of 'system' companies, as indicated by the first problem factor.

The second and third factors reflect problems in market segmentation. Choices of customer types, numbers of customers and their geographical distribution are central issues in segmentation of a market.

Ericsson Business Communications offers relatively large communication systems, that is, systems covering more than 150 extensions. Universities have traditionally expanded geographically and have a need for such communication systems and networks. Such organizations have thus become a major segment for Ericsson Business Communications in Germany. As the number of customers is not too large, the whole of the German market is penetrated. In choosing an appropriate number of customers, however, complementary orders and service requirements must be considered for installed systems.

INTERNATIONAL PRODUCT STANDARDIZATION OR ADAPTATION?

The search for strategic alternatives that pay attention to the balance between products' standardization across a number of user segments and their adaptation to single segments is a central matter which needs to be focused on in empirical research (Humes 1993; Pehrsson 1991, 1993; Prahalad and Doz 1987).

For example, the Satt Control company of Sweden produces equipment for mobile communications and strives for products that can be offered similarly on the global market. However, different legislation requirements and possibilities for receiving permission to use radio frequencies, and varying competitive situations force the company to try to identify strategies covering certain degrees of product adaptation to local markets. What are the alternatives in this choice process?

There exist normative models for developing strategies in general and for the choice between a standardization or an adaptation product policy (see, for example, Usunier 1993). But is there any empirical pattern to be found that can provide experience in balancing product standardization and adaptation to local markets?

Besides presentation of some normative decision models, this section of the chapter presents an empirical survey study (Pehrsson 1995b) that searches for types of business level strategies pertaining to products and markets in terms of users that would differentiate between international businesses operating both in Sweden and Germany. In particular, international product standardization and adaptation is treated. The products under review are industrial products in the similar industries of metal goods, machines and electrotechnical products. The term industrial product means that companies buy and also use the products in question. Products are either components or end products.

Taken literally, international standardization would mean here that

60

identical products would be offered to distinct user segments across national borders. Conversely, adaptation would mean a total lack of common elements, as well as customization and localization of the offer in order to meet regional requirements.

Standardization means the possibility of coordinating activities across segments and reducing costs, whereas adaptation implies the possibility of adjusting the offer by customizing and/or localizing it in order to satisfy local needs. If adaptation goes too far, it may be difficult to achieve scale effects in various functions. On the other hand, total standardization means vulnerability to price competition. In fact, standardization and adaptation of the offer is a matter of degree (Boddewyn et al. 1986; Buzzell 1968; Pehrsson 1993; Quelch and Hoff 1986; Sorenson and Wiechmann 1975).

Although there exist good examples of earlier research concerning typologies of business strategies to be used in general contexts (e.g. Chrisman et al. 1988; Galbraith and Schendel 1983; Porter 1980), as well as in global industry contexts (Doz 1986; Hamel and Prahalad 1985; Jolly 1988; Morrison and Roth 1992), these typologies usually consist of strategies that have to be broken down in order to treat the standardization/adaptation dilemma.

A similar difficulty is inherent in the utilization of business level strategies in the global industries of, for example, Morrison and Roth (1992). In an ambitious effort empirically to develop strategy types, the authors define the term 'global industry' and study eleven manufacturing and consumer goods industries that can be classified as global. The study results in four global strategy types:

1 domestic product specialization;
2 exporting high-quality offers;
3 international product innovation;
4 quasi-global combination strategy.

The validity of such strategies depends heavily on the intricate matter of defining a 'global industry'.

In my opinion research must be even more inductively oriented and should therefore start by exploring the patterns of business level strategies as regards businesses competing in at least two separate local markets. Should a pattern of business level strategies emerge in comparing two markets, research can then go forward, expanding the number of markets that are to be scrutinized.

When it comes to survey studies, which are necessary in the search for patterns, pioneering studies of rather broad categories such as industrial and consumer goods companies have been carried out (e.g. Galbraith and Schendel 1983; Morrison and Roth 1992). However, researchers like Walters (1986) emphasize particularly that some confusion arises from the diversity of the products' characteristics under review in the surveys.

The major body of the literature on standardization and adaptation has been concerned with international promotional policy (Walters 1986). Keegan (1969) widened the scope of the discussion and investigated product and communication policies. This was done, however, on the basis of a few casual observations. Keegan was followed by researchers like Samiee and Roth (1992) who investigated performance levels of high and low standardization companies. Despite these efforts, thorough studies of international product policies are missing.

Thus, studies of product strategies of businesses operating in one industry or similar industries, as well as studies relying on more than just a few casual observations, are lacking and need to be carried out in order to extend our understanding of international business strategies.

Consequently, three types of international business strategies emerge in the study (Pehrsson 1995b): business concentration, product adaptation and user divergence. In the business concentration strategy, one emphasizes similarities across national boundaries, regarding both user characteristics and product design. As regards the user divergence strategy, standardization concerns only the product. In product adaptation, an effort both to localize the product and to customize it is present to satisfy local needs.

The study reveals a pattern of strategies concerning international businesses competing in two separate local markets. The discussed strategy types refer particularly to international product standardization and adaptation, but they need to be further developed and also explained by extending the number of markets to be studied. By applying such an inductively oriented research approach, we may establish the types of global business strategies focusing on the standardization/adaptation dilemma that could be assessed in strategy choice processes.

Applied measurements in a two-country study

From the discussion above it transpires that the following exploratory research question is appropriate for an empirical study: Can any pattern of business strategies be noticed, in terms of how businesses treat international product standardization and adaptation, that distinguishes international businesses operating in two local markets? In the survey study[2] I searched for a pattern by examining the degrees of product and user similarities between the local markets of Sweden and Germany. In accordance with the research question, the following section initially presents the frame of reference for measuring the degree of product and user similarity between different local markets.

Degree of product similarity between local markets

Before measuring the degree of similarity of a product programme on different local markets, it is necessary to define the characteristics of a product programme. A number of ways exist in which product programmes can be characterized (e.g. Toyne and Walters 1989; Usunier 1993). Toyne and Walters characterize industrial product programmes in the following manner: product attributes (design, performance characteristics, quality, other features), pre-sales services (delivery quality), post-sales services (operating advice, repair and maintenance), packaging, labelling, brands and warranties. Usunier presents product, symbolic and service attributes.

Given the exploratory nature of this study, it is important to try to capture the degree of product similarity between local markets using common and measurable characteristics of industrial products, while other attributes might be used in future research. The term product is defined in its broad sense and consists of physical products and appurtenant non-material services, and the following characteristics will be used:

- product attributes (design, functional performance, areas of use, complementary products offered by the same supplier);
- services (delivery quality – delivery speed and safety – and operating advice and services);
- legislation requirements.

The characteristics regarding product attributes and services stem from Toyne and Walters (1989). Besides design, every industrial product can be characterized by functional performance and an area of use. These attributes correspond to Toyne and Walters' performance characteristics. Frequently, the core of an industrial product is complemented by other products offered by the same supplier and this is also an important attribute. Attributes of product quality are generally very difficult to measure and will not be included in this study.

Pre-sales services will be characterized in this study by delivery quality, which is specified in terms of delivery speed and safety, while post-sales services include operating advice and services. Packaging, labelling, brands and warranties are not included in this study, since such characteristics are judged not to be a part of the core of industrial products and also to a large extent symbolic in nature. This means that they are difficult to measure.

The characteristic in this study pertaining to legislation requirements originates from the work of Sorenson and Wiechmann (1975). In different countries, legislation bans different product features and distribution services for a given physical product. Each of these factors might necessitate a mandatory change (Albaum *et al.* 1989) in a company's business approach depending on the country concerned. Such obligatory product adaptation should be distinguished from voluntary adaptation in which a company chooses to make changes to the product in response to the existing local market conditions.

Degree of user similarity between local markets

From the theoretical point of view, a central consideration in pursuing international business strategies involves market definition and perhaps also customer segmentation. Similarities between customers from different local markets, and in particular the effects that the similarities have on standardization and adaptation decisions, have been discussed by Douglas and Wind (1987), Jain (1989), Porter (1986) and others.

In this exploratory study, I will try to measure the degrees of customer similarity between local markets in the following manner. As industrial market segmentation is normally valid for product users and not for intermediaries, the characteristics of the using companies operating in different local markets are the focal point of the study:

- Demographic characteristics (the location of users in terms of industries, the size of using companies in terms of turnover).
- Operating characteristics (users' experience of the product, users' general competence).
- Purchasing characteristics (users' buying routines, users' normal order sizes).
- Situational characteristics (users' requirements of delivery quality, users' need for specialty products).
- Competition characteristics (the number of competing offers from which the users can choose).

The above characteristics, except the one concerning competition, constitute the segmentation model of Bonoma and Shapiro (1983), where they have been proposed for the segmentation of industrial markets. According to the authors, demographic characteristics constitute the most important segmentation base, the main reason being that demographic information is the most easily available. Demographic information has also been used as a segmentation base in, for instance, the study by Sorenson and Wiechmann (1975).

Although a company which focuses on segments rather than on the whole market can be more efficient than its competitors, competition has to be taken into consideration when it comes to segmentation. The model of Flodhammar (1977) contains the competition component in the form of a number of alternative offers from which a buying company may choose. Notwithstanding the fact that competition in a broad sense includes possible substitutes, these are not taken into consideration.

Strategic alternatives generated in the study: business concentration, product adaptation and user divergence

In the two-country study three types of international business strategies have appeared: business concentration, product adaptation and user divergence. These strategies pertain to industrial products and markets in terms of users, and distinguish international businesses operating in both Sweden and Germany.

All three strategy types reflect businesses' treatment of international standardization and adaptation. In the business concentration strategy, one emphasizes similarities across national boundaries when considering both user characteristics and product design. Thus, businesses following this strategy seem either explicitly or implicitly to apply international standardization quite literally. The advantages of this strategy may consist of uniform development of the products and communication with the users.

When it comes to the user divergence strategy, a standardization effort applies to the product itself. Here, one probably tries to exploit scale effects in production and to save costs. Business level managers involved in strategy formulation for this type of business also have to pay considerable attention to uniform product development and global competitors. This means that strategy formulation is carried out to a large extent in a centralized manner. But as user characteristics diverge between the local markets, it is probably difficult fully to coordinate marketing activities. In particular, the different sizes of the using companies and their regular order sizes imply that the businesses' bargaining power generally varies between countries and this makes the formulation of marketing programmes intricate.

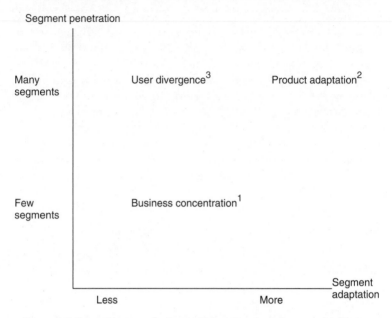

Figure 3.2 Strategy types referring to international product standardization and adaptation.

Notes:
1 User segments that cross national borders, similar product design
2 Users in different industries, product customization and localization
3 Users in the same industries but of different sizes, similar products

Adaptation pertaining to both localizing the product and customizing it in order to fulfil local needs is particularly noticeable in the product adaptation strategy. Although here one tries to gain advantages by distinguishing the offer from those of competitors in a decentralized manner, extreme adaptation is an obstacle to international coordination. In this section of the chapter, the three types of international business strategies identified in the study will be discussed more deeply. Figure 3.2 positions the strategies in the strategic states model.

Strategy type 1: business concentration

The first strategy type accounting for 46 per cent of the sample (n = 56), appears as a strategy of business concentration. This cluster of businesses emphasizes most strongly the similarities in user characteristics and product design. Businesses applying this strategy type seem to search for pure user segments that cross the national boundaries and can be penetrated by products of similar design.

The existence of relatively homogeneous segments in this strategy type is further manifested by similarities as regards the users' experience and their regular order size. Businesses pursuing a concentration strategy also agree to a large extent that users in Sweden and Germany have an equal number of competing offers from which to choose. This means that in these respects the using companies are generally similar.

No major differences in legislation requirements are perceived between Sweden and Germany, which facilitates the marketing of similar products to a rather homogeneous user segment.

In the simplest case, the business unit selects a single user segment that crosses the national boundaries. Abell (1980) lists a number of viable reasons behind a single-segment concentration strategy. The business might have a natural match to the segment's key success requirements; it might have very limited funds and can operate only in one segment; it might be a segment with no other competitors; it might be a segment that is a logical launching pad for further segment expansion. Through concentrated marketing, the business achieves a strong market position in the segment owing to its greater knowledge of the needs of users in the segment, and the special reputation it builds. Furthermore, the business enjoys many operating economies through specializing its production, distribution and promotion. If it niches well in the segment, the business can earn a high return on its investment.

Following the strategic states model presented in this book, concentrated marketing involves higher than normal risks. The demand in the particular market segment can decrease, or a competitor may decide to enter the same segment.

The strategy of the Antenna company group is an example of a business concentration strategy. This group produces and offers terminal-connected antennas for cars, boats and portable radio sets. A subsidiary in Sweden develops, produces and brings antennas to this market. In Germany, antennas are distributed by a wholly owned sales subsidiary. The customers could be divided into two groups: (a) telephone manufacturers and major distributors; (b) domestic dealers and installation contractors. These customer groups assume the character of cross-border segments and customers of a segment are penetrated similarly, whether located in Sweden or Germany. The antennas are of a standardized nature and can be connected to most of the existing mobile telephones in cars and boats, and hand-portable telephones.

Strategy type 2: product adaptation

About 27 per cent of the sample (thirty-two businesses) belongs to the second cluster which represents a strategy of product adaptation. Here, the main products offered on the Swedish market are designed slightly differently from those designed for the German market. To some extent differences in the design of the main products can be explained by a need to adapt product features to varying legislative requirements. Consequently, the adaptation of the design of the main products to local conditions is a manifestation of a rather distinct product adaptation strategy.

However, this product adaptation strategy consists not only of a localizing component, but also contains a certain degree of customizing. Thus in the second cluster, relatively high divergence between Sweden and Germany concerns the factors of products' areas of use and functional performance. Variations particularly occur regarding users' need of specialty products and requirements concerning delivery quality. Accordingly, the response of the businesses to these differences is to customize the offer by varying products which complement the main product, and varying operating advice and services. This also applies to delivery quality in terms of speed and safety. Furthermore, businesses in this cluster report the most obvious difference between Sweden and Germany regarding users' industry location, which probably implies different areas of use of the products.

A high degree of product adaptation implies a possibility for a business unit to make the offer more unique and to be less dependent on price as a competitive mean. Whether products are adapted to few or many market segments, a number of risks are present. In accordance with the strategic states model, one obvious risk is that adaptation means that products cannot easily be available to customers in other market segments. The risk becomes particularly high if the business unit penetrates only one segment and the focused customers suddenly reduce their purchases.

The strategy of the company group of Mobile Telephony Systems is an example of a product adaptation strategy. The company group develops, produces and offers system equipment within the mobile telephony sector. The product range also includes channel filters and monitoring equipment. The subsidiary in Sweden is also responsible for the German market.

A major goal of Mobile Telephony Systems is to become a competitive supplier to the digital mobile telephone system GSM, which will cover all of Europe when fully installed. The customer categories include system suppliers of complete base stations and operators of the installed systems. This segmentation requires close cooperation with the customers on a high technical level. Since demands on technical know-how are very high and customers are not too many, the Swedish subsidiary of Mobile Telephony Systems also takes care of the German market. As channel filters must be adapted to the frequency ranges of each country, the business strategy includes not only customizing, but also a certain degree of localizing.

Strategy type 3: user divergence

The thirty-two businesses in cluster three follow a user divergence strategy. The main products offered in Sweden and Germany are fairly similar when it comes to product design, functional performance and areas of use.

User characteristics are, however, different in the two countries. Differences appear primarily in the size of the using companies and their regular order size. In most cases, German customers are probably larger than the Swedish ones. Despite varying turnover of using companies, users in Sweden tend to be located in the same industries as the ones in Germany.

This strategy assumes the character of product specialization, and a business unit can build up a strong reputation in the specific product area. A serious threat occurs, however, if the product technology is supplanted by an emerging substitute technology.

The Steel company's strategy is an illustrative example in this respect. The company produces and offers advanced steel products such as hot rolled heavy plate in various thicknesses and dimensions. These products are used for the manufacture of heavy machinery, earthmoving equipment, storage tanks, pipelines and ships. The main part of the production is exported through sales companies in Denmark, Norway, Finland, Great Britain, France, Germany, the Netherlands, Belgium and the USA.

One searches for customers of the same character and emphasizes reliable deliveries. Such deliveries make it possible for a customer to reduce his own stocks and therefore the amount of money tied up. The company has developed an advanced computer system to optimize all processes of production and distribution. The mill is entirely vertically integrated, which means that management has complete control over the production process. A large amount of resources are spent on research and development of the production process and the products.

Decision models concerning international product standardization and adaptation

There exist normative models that might help when it comes to decisions on international product standardization and adaptation. This section will present two models: a framework elaborated by Usunier (1993) which specifically focuses on product decisions, and the more comprehensive model of Prahalad and Doz (1987). The latter model has implications for the design of international organizations.

Usunier introduces a rather detailed framework for the choice between pure product standardization and adaptation based on product attributes. A product can be defined as a set of attributes which provide the purchaser or user with actual benefits. According to Usunier there are three layers of attributes:

1 The physical attributes (size, weight, colour, etc.). Standardization of these attributes affords the greatest potential for cost benefits since economies of scale are made principally at the manufacturing stage.
2 Service attributes (maintenance, after-sales service, spare parts availability, etc.). These attributes are fairly difficult to standardize, as circumstances for service delivery differ widely from one country to another. It should further be emphasized that most services are performed in direct relation to local customers, which means that service attributes are more dependent on culture.
3 Symbolic attributes are often the interpretive element of the physical attributes. A colour is simultaneously a chemical formula for a painting, and also the symbolic meaning conveyed by the material. Symbolic attributes affect the choice between adaptation and standardization in a fairly ambiguous manner. Therefore, when adapting or standardizing symbolic attributes, the requirements for nationalist symbols will intermingle with symbols of exoticism.

According to Usunier, the following arguments are in favour of standardization of physical attributes:

• Experience effects/scale savings. The effects, and accordingly the cost reductions related to cumulated production, clearly weigh in favour of standardization.
• International standards, international product use and international diffusion of innovations. Although technical standards largely originate in individual countries, there are industries where international

standards tend to develop. Furthermore, some products achieve 'international usage' and innovative products often experience an international diffusion process. Large research and development (R&D) expenses are initially incurred for many innovative products, which are not greatly affected by culture. The pace of diffusion of innovations is largely enhanced by the strength of the groups of 'early adopters'.

As regards physical attributes, the following arguments are in favour of adaptation:

- Opportunity to supply adaptations which result in a reduction in costs. Supply of an adapted product, corresponding to the local demand, can lead to a sufficient reduction in costs to compensate for the loss in cumulated volume. This situation is, however, rare. There are some examples of 'simplified' cars or 'simplified' computers designed for developing countries.
- Technical standard, hygiene and safety regulations, consumption trends, climate and physical environment. Compulsory adaptation for the physical attributes is often related to national regulation and standards such as industrial standards for electrical supply. Safety standards are common in the motor industry, etc.

The following arguments are in favour of standardizing service attributes:

- Learning effects are significant. There can be substantial learning effects with service attributes. For example, various management procedures such as stocking of spare parts or hotel laundering may be standardized.
- 'Mobile' clientele. Service standardization will be required when the clientele is internationally 'mobile' and customers move with their service requirements.

Finally, when it comes to adaptation of service attributes, there are some other pressures:

- Differences in service conditions or distribution networks. Service requirements differ widely from country to country because they are related to environmental factors such as the level of technical expertise, the level of labour costs, climatic differences, etc. Services are generally performed by delegation to distribution channels. The shortage of available and/or adequate channels and the small size of the outlets are an obstacle to services, particularly in developing countries.

- Opportunity to supply services that are far less comprehensive than in the country of origin. In certain cases the adaptation of service attributes will lead to cost savings because locally supplied services will be far less comprehensive than in the country of origin. This is feasible either when local service requirements are less demanding or when the product has been expressly constructed to be almost maintenance free.

Prahalad and Doz (1987) present another model that can be applied to facilitate strategy choices pertaining to international product standardization and adaptation. Three building blocks are present in the model: global integration of activities, global strategic coordination and local responsiveness. The blocks refer to the nature of relationships between headquarters and subsidiaries, as well as among subsidiaries in a multinational setting. However, those relationships are dependent on the nature of the business units in the diversified multinationals. The economic, technological and competitive characteristics of a business enable us to define pressures for global integration of activities and local responsiveness. The need for strategic coordination is harder to focus. Typically, businesses that need significant global integration of activities also require strategic coordination. However, given active global competition locally responsive business units may demand strategic coordination as well.

Integration in the context of Prahalad and Doz (1987) refers to the centralized management of geographically dispersed activities on an ongoing basis. Managing shipments of parts and subassemblies across a network of manufacturing facilities in various countries is an example of integration activities.

The need for integration arises in response to pressures to reduce costs and optimize investments. Such pressures may force location of plants in countries with low labour costs, such as South Korea, Taiwan and Malaysia. Products are then shipped from those plants to the established markets of the USA, Europe or elsewhere. The same pressures may also lead to building large highly specialized plants, to realize economies of scale. Managerially, this translates into a need for ongoing management of logistics that cut across multiple national boundaries. To achieve successful international product standardization in principle requires a high degree of integration.

Strategic coordination refers to the central management of resource commitments across national boundaries in the pursuit of a strategy. It is distinct from the integration of ongoing activities across national borders. Typical examples would involve coordinating R&D priorities

72

across several laboratories, coordinating pricing to global customers, and facilitating transfers of technology from headquarters to subsidiaries and across subsidiaries. Unlike activity integration, strategic coordination can be selective and nonroutine.

The goal of strategic coordination is to recognize, build, and defend long-term competitive advantages. For example, headquarters may assign highly differentiated goals to various subsidiaries in the same business unit in order to develop a coherent response to competition. Strategic coordination, like integration of activities, often involves headquarters and one or several subsidiaries. Coordination decisions transcend a single subsidiary.

According to Prahalad and Doz (1987), local responsiveness refers to resource commitment decisions taken autonomously by a subsidiary in response to primarily local competitive or customer demands. In a wide variety of businesses, there may be no competitive advantage to be gained by coordinating actions across subsidiaries. Typically, businesses where there are no meaningful economies of scale or proprietary technology fall into this category. The need for significant local adaptation of products or differences in distribution across national markets may also indicate a need for local responsiveness.

The authors suggest that we can use the following criteria for evaluating the pressures for global coordination and integration as well as local responsiveness. The pressures regarding each criterion can be measured on a three-point scale, where the values represent high, medium or low.

Pressures for global strategic coordination

- *Importance of multinational customers*: the dependence of a business unit on multinational Original Equipment Manufacturers (OEM) imposes a need for coordination. Multinational customers can and often do compare prices charged by their suppliers around the world; they will also demand the same level of service and product support wherever they are based. The product is often sold at the centre and delivered around the world, wherever the multinational customer may need it.
- *Presence of multinational competitors*: the presence of competitors who operate in multiple markets indicates the potential for global competition. Consequently, it is crucial to be ready to respond to their actions wherever most appropriate. The presence of multinational competitors calls for global strategic coordination.

- *Investment intensity*: if an aspect of the business is investment intensive (e.g. R&D or manufacturing), the need to leverage that investment increases the need for global coordination. Worldwide product strategies have to be developed and implemented quickly to make the large initial investments profitable.

Pressures for global integration

- *Technology intensity*: technology intensity and the extent of proprietary technology often encourage firms to manufacture in only a few selected locations. Having fewer manufacturing sites allows easier control over quality, cost and new product introduction. Centralized product development and manufacturing operations in a few locations result in global integration, particularly when the markets are widely dispersed.
- *Pressure for cost reduction*: global integration is often a response to pressure for cost reduction. Cost reduction requires sourcing the product from low factor cost locations (global sourcing), or exploiting economies of scale and experience by building large plants which serve multiple national markets. Either approach to lowering costs imposes a need for global integration.
- *Universal needs*: if the product meets a universal need and requires little adaptation across national markets, global integration is obviously facilitated.
- *Access to raw materials and energy*: access to raw materials and a cheap and plentiful supply of energy can force manufacturing to be located in a specific area.

Pressures for local responsiveness

- *Differences in customer needs*: businesses that thrive on satisfying a diverse set of customer needs, most of which is nation or region specific, require a locally responsive strategy.
- *Differences in distribution channels*: differences in distribution channels in various countries and the differences in pricing, product positioning, promotion, and advertising which those differences entail indicate the need for local responsiveness.
- *Availability of substitutes and the need to adapt*: if a product function is being met by local substitutes, with differing price-performance relationships in a given national market, or if the product must be significantly adapted to be locally competitive, then a locally responsive strategy is indicated.

- *Market structure:* market structure includes the importance of local competitors as compared to multinational ones, as well as the extent of their concentration. If local competitors tend to control a significant portion of the market and/or if the industry is not concentrated, then a locally responsive posture is most usually indicated. A fragmented industry with local competitors indicates that there may be no inherent advantages to size and scale, unless product and process technology can be changed.
- *Host government demands:* demands imposed by host governments for local self-sufficiency for a variety of reasons – from concerns of national development to concerns of national security – can force a business to become locally responsive.

The three strategic alternatives dealing with international standardization and adaptation that were presented earlier in this chapter (business concentration, product adaptation and user divergence) were exemplified by the strategies of (a) the Antenna company group; (b) the company group of Mobile Telephony Systems; (c) the Steel company respectively. Each of these businesses is subject to a different combination of pressures toward global coordination and local responsiveness. The differences can be identified by using the discussed criteria (Table 3.7).

The characteristics of the businesses can be captured in an integration–responsiveness grid (Prahalad and Doz 1987), as shown in Figure 3.3. Classifying businesses broadly as either global or local can be misleading. There are few businesses which can be considered as exclusively local. If there were no advantages to be gained from such a business by a multinational company, then the business would be likely to become very fragmented with no scope for advancing knowledge, products, financial muscle, or brands across markets. On the other hand, few businesses can be considered as totally global. A variety of factors, including the need for a responsive and differentiated local presence in various countries, make it difficult completely to ignore the demands of various national markets. The purpose of the framework in question is to assess the relative importance of the two sets of conflicting demands that companies have to struggle against and to determine which of the two provides strategic leverage at a given point in time.

Following the example of Prahalad and Doz, several managerial conclusions can be drawn from mapping the characteristics of a business on the integration–responsiveness grid.

Steel products, which require strong global integration and show a low demand for local responsiveness, suggest that managers involved in

Table 3.7 Pressures for global strategic coordination, global integration and local responsiveness: comparison of two businesses

Criteria	Mobile telephony systems	Steel products
Pressures for global strategic coordination		
Importance of multinational customers	Low	Medium
Presence of multinational competitors	Low	High
Investment intensity	Medium	High
Pressures for global integration	Medium	High
Technology intensity	High	High
Pressure for cost reduction	Low	High
Universal needs	Low	Medium
Access to raw materials and energy	NA	High
Pressures for local responsiveness	High	Low
Differences in customer needs	High	Medium
Differences in distribution	Medium	Low
Availability of substitutes and need to adapt	High	Medium
Market structure	Fragmented	Concentrated
Host government demands	NA	NA

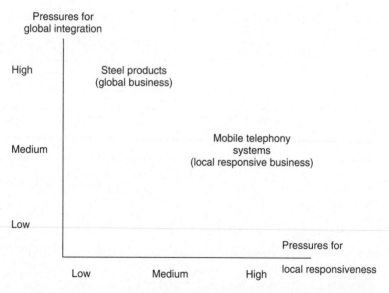

Figure 3.3 Integration–responsiveness grid: characteristics of two businesses

76

strategic planning for this kind of business must pay much more attention to such aspects as economies of scale, product development, global customers, and global competitors rather than to issues that have to do with local responsiveness. This also implies that decisions concerning resource allocation with respect to the key elements of the strategy applied to this kind of business (such as plant location and investment, pricing, product development and key account management) may have to be centralized. In other words, in the steel business, the locus of strategic management is constituted in the central worldwide responsible management group.

On the other hand, for Mobile Telephony Systems, the key strategic choices (pricing, promotion, choice of channels) have to be managed at least theoretically in a decentralized mode, following the product adaptation strategy. The centre for strategy-making would be formed by the regional or the national subsidiary managers.

In both businesses representing the two strategy extremes (the Steel company and the company group of Mobile Telephony Systems), managers can make relatively clear-cut choices of what aspects of the business to leverage. Therefore, a reasonably straightforward organizational form is possible: worldwide business management in the case of steel products and area management in the case of Mobile Telephony.

When it comes to businesses that fall between the two extremes, the strategic choice is not all that clear-cut. Some strategic elements, like plant size and the choice of technology, may have to be managed centrally. On the other hand, deliveries, competitors, and some of the key customers may have to be managed both regionally and locally. This implies that managers must focus their attention simultaneously on those aspects of business that require global integration and on those that demand local responsiveness, as well as on the varying degrees of strategic coordination. This need for multiple focal points of management suggests that managers must reflect the need for multiple points of view – the need to integrate and at the same time the need to be responsive to the way in which business is organized. This requires the organization to be multifocal or of the matrix type.

EVALUATION OF STRATEGIC ALTERNATIVES

Before a company or business unit evaluates strategic alternatives it is necessary to determine criteria against which each option can be judged. However, even the most thorough strategy evaluation cannot possibly anticipate all the detailed problems which might occur in the implementation of a selected business strategy. So it is necessary to recognize that a business strategy will often have to be constantly revised and developed.

Of the many tests that could justifiably be applied to a business strategy, Rumelt (1980) argues that most will fit within one of these broad criteria:

- consistency – the strategy must not present mutually inconsistent goals and policies;
- consonance – the strategy must represent an adaptive response to the external environment and to the critical changes occurring within it;
- advantage – the strategy must provide for the creation and/or maintenance of a competitive advantage in the selected area of activity;
- feasibility – the strategy must neither overtax available resources nor create unsolvable subproblems.

Johnson and Scholes (1993) add acceptability as another criterion. Acceptability is strongly related to people's expectations, and therefore the issue of 'acceptable to whom' requires the analysis to be thought through carefully.

According to Rumelt (1980), the business strategy must not present mutually inconsistent goals and policies. Gross inconsistency within a strategy seems unlikely until it is realized that many strategies have not been explicitly formulated but have evolved over time in an ad hoc fashion. Even strategies that are the result of formal procedures may easily contain compromise arrangements between opposing power groups. Rumelt continues to say that a key function of strategy is to provide coherence to organizational action. A clear and explicit strategy choice can foster a climate of tacit coordination that is more efficient than most administrative routines. If management does not make a clear choice of, for example, where the company stands on the question of international market segmentation, there will be continuing conflict between various organizational functions.

When it comes to consonance, the way in which a business relates to its environment has two aspects: the business must both match and be adapted to its environment, and it must at the same time compete with other firms that are also trying to adapt. This dual character of the relationship between the firm and its environment has its analog in two different aspects of strategy choice and two different methods of strategy evaluation.

The first aspect of fit deals with the basic mission or scope of the business and the second with its special competitive position. Analysis of the first is normally done by looking at changing economic and social conditions over time. Analysis of the second typically focuses on the differences across firms at a given time.

Rumelt (1980) says that one major difficulty in evaluating consonance is that most of the critical threats to a business are those that come from without, threatening an entire group of firms. Management, however, is often so engrossed in competitive thinking that such threats are only recognized after the damage has reached considerable proportions. Thus, the key to evaluating consonance is an understanding of why the business exists at all and how it assumed its current character. Once the analyst obtains a good grasp of the basic foundation that supports and defines the business, it is possible to study the consequences of key trends and changes. Without such an understanding, there is no good way of deciding what kinds of changes are most crucial, and the analyst can quickly be overwhelmed with data.

The third criterion highlights advantage and relies on an assessment of differences among firms. Competitive advantages can normally be traced to one of these roots: superior resources, superior skills, or superior position. The first two represent the ability of a business to do more and do it better than its rivals. The critical analytical issue here is the question of which skills and resources represent advantages.

Positional advantage can be gained by foresight, superior skill or resources, or just plain luck. Once gained, a good position is defensible. This means that it returns enough value to warrant its continued maintenance and would be so costly to capture that rivals are deterred from attacks on the core of the business. The types of positional advantage that are most well known are those associated with size or scale. However, the principal characteristic of good position is that it permits the firm to obtain advantage from policies that would not similarly benefit rivals without that position.

The final broad test of business strategy is its feasibility. Can the strategy be implemented successfully with the resources available? The financial resources of a business are normally the easiest to quantify and are often the first limitation against which strategy is tested. The less quantifiable but actually more rigid limitation on strategy choice is that imposed by the individual and organizational capabilities available. In assessing the organization's ability to carry out a strategy, Rumelt (1980) suggests three questions to be asked:

1 Has the organization demonstrated that it possesses the problem-solving abilities and/or special competences required by the strategy?

2 Has the organization demonstrated the degree of coordinative and integrative skill necessary to carry out the strategy?

3 Does the strategy challenge and motivate key personnel, and is it acceptable to those who must lend their support?

Johnson and Scholes (1993) regard acceptability as a specific evaluation criterion, and emphasize that the issue of 'acceptable to whom' needs to be carefully discussed. As a basis for such a discussion they suggest these questions:

1 Will any proposed changes be appropriate to the general expectations within the organization?

2 Will the function of any department, group or individual change significantly?

3 Will the organization's relationships with outside stakeholders need to change?

4 Will the strategy be acceptable in the organization's environment (e.g. will the local community accept it)?

NOTES

1 I carried out the exploratory study (Pehrsson 1993) in 1991. Mail questionnaires were used to collect cross-sectional data concerning degrees of problems in strategy choices. The sample consisted of 238 Swedish subsidiaries that marketed metal goods, machines or electrotechnical products in West Germany in 1989. Based on information from the companies, they were divided by me into two categories: companies that mainly offer separate products and companies that mainly offer systems of products. In total, 103 companies finally answered the questionnaire representing a response rate of 44 per cent. The turnover in 1990 of the companies that answered the questionnaire varied between DM1 million and DM460 million. The median turnover was around DM30 million.

A total of nine characteristics of the components of business strategy presented in this chapter defines the variables or items in the questionnaire. The presidents of the companies in the sample were asked to rate the extent to which they consider each item as a problem in contemporary strategy choices of their companies in the German market. Ratings were made on five-point Likert scales, with one representing 'very small problem' and five representing 'very large problem', and the items are: to choose breadth of product range; to choose varieties of customer types; to choose numbers of customers; to choose geographical regions; to choose degrees of product customization; to choose degrees of product standardization; to choose product qualities; to choose price levels; and to choose cost levels.

The 'product' companies reported that, on average, 45 per cent of their deliveries were customized, while 95 per cent of the delivered systems of the 'system' companies were tailored specifically to each customer.

Companies in the latter category typically complement physical products by construction engineering, relatively extensive customer education and other services.

A total of sixty companies mainly considered themselves as offering separate products, such as components for spinning machines, fastening components, pneumatic tools, precision tools for metal processing, hobby tools, bearings of various types, dosage equipment, balance electronics, industrial centrifuges, neon signs, radiators for electrical devices, industrial cranes, office lamps and components for industrial pumps.

A total of forty-three companies mainly regarded themselves as offering systems of products, such as constructions and devices for milk processing, refrigeration plants, systems for refuse recycling, hydraulic systems, driving systems for paper machines, computerized welding machines, constructions for pumping stations and turbines, pneumatic and hydraulic mobile systems, products for medical dialysis treatment, optical measuring systems and ventilation constructions.

Multivariate analysis was applied to search for statistically significant differences between the two company categories, to calculate correlations among variables for each category and to search for underlying factor structures.

Four statistically significant differences (chi-square tests) exist between the two types of companies, indicating a contingency effect regarding strategy choices. A significant difference at the 99 per cent confidence level appeared for 'to choose degrees of product standardization', while significant differences at the 95 per cent confidence level appeared for 'to choose breadth of product range', 'to choose degrees of product customization' and 'to choose product qualities'.

As all these differences are valid for product choices, the disparity between the company categories in the study seems to be enough to venture the hypothesis that the degree of problems in strategy choices perceived by 'product' companies deviates from the degree of problems perceived by 'system' companies.

Correlation analysis of variables in strategy choices showed relatively high correlation coefficients and there seemed to be multicollinearity.

Consequently, I searched for underlying factor structures and found three factors that represent variables for each company category. Each factor was labelled according to the content of the variable that dominates that particular factor. For 'product' companies, factors that could be labelled 'to choose product qualities', 'to choose cost levels', and 'to choose customer types' were formed. For 'system' companies, factors were named 'to choose product qualities', 'to choose numbers of customers', and 'to choose geographical regions'.

2 The population of the quantitative study reported in Pehrsson (1995b) consists of Swedish business units that manufacture industrial products in the similar industries of metal goods, machines and electrotechnical products. The main products of the business units are offered for sale through the parent company in Sweden or through subsidiaries both in Sweden and in Germany.

According to the Export Register set up by the Swedish Trade Council, there were 221 business units representing 221 firms in the population in 1993. All subsidiaries in Germany were responsible for at least sales on that market. Some of the subsidiaries were also engaged in local manufacturing, design, and so on.

The respondents hold positions such as president, general manager and marketing director, and they are responsible for the main products of the businesses. The 221 respondents in 1993 received a mail questionnaire. In total, 120 businesses returned the questionnaire, representing a response rate of 54 per cent. The analysis of the information in the Register regarding the business units which did not reply indicated that these did not differ significantly from the responding units when it comes to product types. Therefore, the products offered by the responding businesses may be considered to be representative for the entire population.

The respondents were asked to rate the extent to which they consider seven aspects of the main product (i.e. seven variables) similar in the Swedish and the German markets respectively. These variables were: product design, the product's functional performance, areas of use, complementary products, delivery quality, operating advice and service, and legislation requirements. Ratings were made on five-point Likert scales, with one representing 'totally similar' and five representing 'totally dissimilar'. The same procedure was applied to measure the extent to which the respondents agreed with nine statements. These variables concerned similarities between Swedish and German using companies of the businesses' main products: industry location, turnover, product experience, general competence, buying routines, normal order sizes, requirements on delivery quality, need for specialty products, and numbers of competing offers to choose from. On these Likert scales, one represented 'strongly approve', implying a high degree of similarity between the users in Sweden and Germany, and five represented 'strongly disapprove', or a high degree of dissimilarity.

The main purpose of the study was to try to group business units into homogeneous clusters of units according to the type of international business strategy which they followed. To further facilitate the interpretation of the results, the number of strategy variables (16) was first reduced through the application of factor analysis, using the matrix of variable correlations as the input. The analysis resulted in four strategy factors: user characteristics, areas of use, products' functional performance and product design. A cluster analysis method was then applied, using the four strategy factors as the input. Clusters of business units were identified by analysing the factor score means, and this resulted in three types of international business strategies: business concentration (56 businesses), product adaptation (32) and user divergence (32). Furthermore, group differences on single strategy variables were analysed in order to supply the interpretation of each cluster. Chi-square tests confirmed that cluster differences on the variables are statistically significant.

Part II

DEVELOPMENT
OF INTERNATIONAL
BUSINESS STRATEGIES
IN THE
TELECOMMUNICATIONS
INDUSTRY

4

THE TELECOMMUNICATIONS INDUSTRY

Telecommunications and computer technology are important parts of the growing area of information technology. Telecommunications make possible the building of widespread computer systems. These enable communication locally and more widely, both in analog and digital environments.

Telecommunications equipment and services, maintenance, support and office equipment are normally referred to as the foundation for the telecommunications industry. Telecommunications equipment consists of telephones, switching equipment, transmission equipment, receiver terminals, line and other equipment. The number of telecommunications services (call charges, leased lines, switching services and so on) is constantly increasing, and mobile communications is the fastest growing area.

Public telecommunications involves equipment and services for local calls, domestic long-distance calls and international calls using public networks, as opposed to company or private networks. Communications may use either stationary telephones or mobile ones.

Besides subscriber telephones, a mobile telephony network consists of radio base stations which communicate with the telephones using antennas located on high places. These stations are linked to switching systems by different types of cables.

Telephone exchanges are usually classified according to the area of application. A distinction is thus made between public exchanges, such as Ericsson's AXE system, and exchanges for office use. The definition of small versus large subscriber exchanges for office use is somewhat vague, but exchanges with fewer than fifty extensions could be defined as small exchanges and those with more than fifty extensions could be defined as large exchanges. Small exchanges are referred to as Key systems and can often be placed beside a telephone apparatus. The large exchanges go under the name of the Public Automatic Branch Exchange (PABX). In standard applications a PABX handles not only the regular telephone traffic, but also data and telecommunications.

Boundaries within the telecommunications area are continuously changing. Public networks are now able to provide services which were earlier provided only by private networks. At the same time private exchanges serving the offices of various companies and organizations are becoming more efficient in linking together geographically widely spread units. This makes the division between the areas of public and private telecommunications less clear, and applies likewise to the division between stationary communication systems using cables and those using radios.

This chapter presents two major changes in the telecommunications industry: the deregulation process which takes place in and between countries and facilitates new entrants to establish themselves in the industry. The evolution of mobile telephony is also briefly described, as this area is a fast-growing part of the industry. Finally, the major actors in the industry (suppliers of equipment and systems, network operators, retailers and end-users) are presented. Here, both company cases and surveys are put forward as examples.

CHANGES IN THE TELECOMMUNICATIONS INDUSTRY

A number of processes are taking place which are gradually changing the character of the telecommunications industry. A far-reaching deregulation process is in progress which is opening up the industry for new entrants and extending the supply in markets for telecommunications. The evolution of mobile telephony is another major change that is having a significant impact on the industry. The introduction of mobility means that for the first time in the history of the telephone, subscribers are not tied to any particular location to make and receive calls.

The deregulation process

It is in the nature of public telephone systems that they have to be adapted to the specific requirements of each individual country. Since the investment costs of such an enterprise can be regarded as rather high and the relationship between the selling and the buying companies is generally of a long-term nature, a country's choice of the basic telephone system is seen as a true marketing challenge.

Telecommunications constitute an important element in a country's infrastructure and are generally provided under governmental auspices or through government-controlled administrations. Such operations are therefore often considered highly important in terms of national employment. This is also why competitive rules concerning telecommunications are decided to a large extent by national governments and parliaments. In all countries there exist restrictions concerning the type of services that are permitted to use the national telecommunications networks.

Europe, North America and Japan have had numerous discussions regarding deregulation. The UK was the first country to begin a comprehensive deregulation process. In 1981 telecommunications activities were separated from the other activities of the post and telecommunications administration, making way for the establishment of British Telecom (BT). The areas concerning apparatus and equipment that were to be connected to the network of BT were also opened to competition by the British government in 1981.

The BT licence of 1984 included more than fifty stringent conditions that would control the market dominance of BT and ensure that it would not abuse its position in a way that would run contrary to the public interest (Bo Rehn, Managing Director, BT Nordic, *Teldok Yearbook 1994*). Among the conditions were:

- An obligation to serve all customers without discrimination or preference, and to provide basic telephony services, and any other services where the demand is reasonable. BT also faces social obligations such as running emergency services.
- An obligation to assist its competitors in pricing announcement rules, interconnection and non-discrimination rules. Interconnection rules compel BT to open up the public networks so that competitors may reach all customers.

In 1984 the government of the USA took a major step towards complete deregulation, abolishing the monopoly of American Telephone and Telegraph (AT&T) for long-distance traffic. AT&T was divided into seven regional companies which were allowed to compete in the areas related to telecommunications such as, for example, the computer area. The American market was also opened up to foreign competitors. The US deregulation resulted in extensive customer benefits:

Customers now have choices of services, service providers, pricing plans, billing and other features, as established carriers and new entrants have responded to customer demand for innovative, efficient, cost-based services. Since 1984, for example, the number of new service offerings that AT&T introduced each year has increased from 35 new offerings in 1985, to 188 new services introduced in 1990. As competitors have kept pace with customer demand, the network capacity of established and new providers has increased, and at the same time, the unit costs of technology have declined. As a result, since 1984, customers have enjoyed significant savings in their telecommunications expenses as market forces have driven prices downward.

(Staffan Reinefjord, Managing Director, AT&T Nordics,
Teldok Yearbook 1994)

The number of new carriers grew rapidly in the first five years after the divestiture of 1 January 1984, with the introduction of interconnection arrangements which allowed customers to access all carriers on an equal basis. During this time, AT&T experienced an annual traffic growth rate of 7.5 per cent. At the same time, the revenues of AT&T's competitors more than quadrupled. The market share of AT&T, based on interstate switched minutes of use, grew from 15.8 per cent prior to the implementation of equal access to 36.7 per cent in 1990. As competitors grew, employment increased with new carriers employing approximately 36,000 persons in 1987 and 47,000 by 1990.

The detailed implementation of a fully competitive long-distance environment in the USA involved a transition period during which specific steps were taken to meet customer and carrier needs. A time-table was established for providing interconnection arrangements and equal access capabilities. In this way, the local operators had a level of certainty from which to consider how these requirements could be included in network modernization and construction plans, while new entrants were provided with a level of certainty to enable them to assess market entry.

In 1987 and 1988 the governments of France and West Germany approved a number of proposals aimed at more intense competition in the telecommunications area. The proposals were meant to facilitate competition in the entire area, except for basic telephony. In these countries, the deregulation process corresponded to the direction taken by the European Community at that time.

Thus, the prior monopolies of France Telecom and Deutsche Bundespost will continue their basic activities in principally the same ways as before. In the early 1990s these organizations were also restructured and the monopolies split into clearly defined organizations, whereas the activities that were expected to meet with competition established subsidiaries.

The governments of France and Germany also want to facilitate competition within the areas of emerging telecommunications services. In Germany private companies will have the possibility of operating networks for mobile telephony and the corresponding services.

All the European Union (EU) countries had existing situations with different types of monopolies for telecommunications services and equipment. The Green Paper of 1987 set the political foundation for a complete liberalization of the terminal market in the widest sense, including all customer equipment. A terminal which is approved in one country should also be able to be used in other member countries. Liberalization of all telecommunications services except 'basic' telephony should also be carried out. Through several legislative acts, the EU has to a large extent accomplished the policies on the formal level, although the actual implementation of directives frequently lags behind (Olof Nordling, Director of EU Affairs, Telia International, *Teldok Yearbook 1994*).

Evolution of mobile telephony systems

The development of the cellular radio capable of accessing the public telephony network was a turning-point in the history of the telephony. For the first time subscribers were not tied to any particular location to make and receive calls. However, during the first years different mobile telephony systems were constructed according to various international standards. This made communication between the existing systems practically impossible.

The only exceptions were the Nordic countries (Denmark, Finland, Norway and Sweden), where the Nordic Mobile Telephony (NMT) system, put into operation in 1981, provided cordless mobile telephone communications in an analog manner between mobile subscribers in the four countries. In 1994 this system was widely used and operational in twenty-eight countries (*Teldok Info*, May, 1994).

Besides NMT a number of analog mobile telephony systems have been developed. The two most widespread are Advanced Mobile Phone System (AMPS), used among other places in North America, and Total Access Communications Systems (TACS), which is operational in countries such as the UK and Italy. As these analog systems are built upon different principles, particular telephones are required for each standard.

In order to set up a uniform standard for mobile telephony in Europe, using the digital technique, a number of countries agreed to choose the Global System for Mobile Communications (GSM) standard. The main events in the development of GSM are as follows:

1982   GSM activities commence.
1986   Field test in France and selection of the access technique.
1988   A memorandum of understanding is signed by eighteen European countries which commit themselves to fulfil the specifications and to start a commercial GSM service in July 1991.
1990   The pre-operational system is put into operation.
1991   The commercial system is introduced.
1992   Coverage of capital cities and airports.
1993   Coverage of main roads.

The aim is to offer free communication within and between all the countries involved. Among other countries, even Australia, India and China will be included as they have decided to adopt the GSM standard. Besides the fact that a subscriber can be reached and make calls within the GSM area, applying a single standard will help to reduce the cost of telephones (usually the case with products which can be manufactured on a larger scale).

By 1994 there existed a further two digital mobile telephony systems: American Digital Cellular (ADC), which has been developed in the USA as a continuation of the analog AMPS, and Japan Digital Cellular (JDC).

ACTORS IN THE TELECOMMUNICATIONS INDUSTRY

Five homogeneous types of actors in the telecommunications industry will be presented here: equipment suppliers, systems suppliers, network operators, retailers and end-users (Figure 4.1). Although the figure separates between the five types, a single company may, in reality, take on more than one role, displaying a number of relations to other actors on the market.

Equipment suppliers provide components and equipment for telephones, exchanges, base stations and networks. There is equipment which constitutes the basis of systems and networks, and other types of equipment, such as mobile telephones, which a customer may buy from a retailer. Many equipment suppliers produce large volumes, as

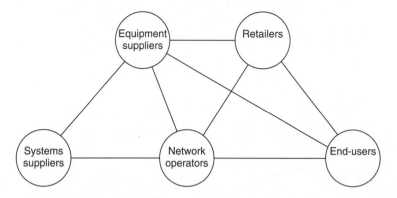

Figure 4.1 Types of actors in the telecommunications industry

obviously the advantages of large-scale production of standardized equipment cannot be disregarded. Ericsson of Sweden, Nokia of Finland, and Motorola of the USA are examples of mobile telephone suppliers. Allgon of Sweden is an example of a supplier of components used in systems building.

Systems suppliers deliver systems exchanges, base stations and networks, mainly to network operators. Examples of systems suppliers can be found among companies such as Ericsson, AT&T of the USA and Siemens of Germany in the area of public telecommunications, and Ericsson, Nokia and Motorola in mobile telephony.

Network operators, such as Telia of Sweden and British Telecom, offer telecommunications services to end-users. A network operator normally has a close relationship with the particular systems supplier who has delivered the network in question, and penetrates end-users both directly and through retailers.

Retailers are frequently local companies consisting of specialists and chains, such as, for example, Teliabutiken in Sweden, which offers telecommunications equipment and services to end-users. These can be classified into three groups: private consumers, companies and other organizations.

The following sections of this chapter will present examples of actors in the focused industry:

1   The Allgon case is an illustration of a relatively small component supplier in mobile telephony.
2   Broader surveys will provide information about systems suppliers in public telecommunications, mobile telephony and office exchanges.

3 Network operators in public telecommunications and mobile telephony will be presented in a broad manner.
4 Strategic groups of retailers on the Swedish mobile telephony market will exemplify a fragmented part of the industry.
5 A survey of buying processes regarding office exchanges will exemplify end-user situations.

Equipment suppliers: a small company's case

The Allgon group of Sweden focuses on antennas, equipment for radio-base stations and mobile telephony appliances (Allgon *Annual Report* 1993). The Systems business area comprises antennas and other equipment for radiobase stations, which means that suppliers of mobile telephony systems and network operators constitute the main customer categories. The remaining business areas of the group include antennas and appliances for mobile telephones.

The activities of the group centre around general technical development, product development, final assembly and distribution, while subcontractors are engaged in manufacturing. All development activities take place at Allgon Antenn AB and Allgon Systems AB, located in Sweden. Allgon Antenn controls three business areas, while Allgon Systems is responsible for its own area. Sales companies have been established in Austria, France, Germany, UK, Singapore and the USA.

The mobile telephony market is characterized by intensive technical progress and volume expansion; at least this was the case in the mid-1990s. New functions and products are constantly introduced on the market. Allgon tries to follow this trend with continuous expansion of its development resources. However, its intention is to stay in the present applications and customer area (i.e. antenna products for mobile telephony). This area is judged to be sufficiently large for a long time to come:

> The market for mobile telephones of the so-called cellular type still expands strongly. Large volumes and more cost efficient solutions imply, however, that the market value will not continue to expand as quickly as the market volume.
>
> The intensive growth will attract capital and new competitors, and sharpen the rivalry. As Allgon belongs to the five dominant companies as regards antennas for mobile telephony systems, our position is strong.

(CEO Per Wejke, Allgon *Annual Report* 1993)

Several new entrants have established themselves as competitors of Allgon Systems. The company's response to.this tendency has been to reduce its dependence on a few major customers, and continue the technical development. A number of new products were introduced in 1993, made possible by the appearance of new network operators in Europe, North America and the Far East.

Systems suppliers: an overview

This section focuses on the supply of switching systems for public networks, both as regards systems for stationary and mobile communications, as well as switching systems for private communications. All these systems rely on electronic technology.

Electronic technology is based on integrated circuits requiring large volumes in order to achieve competitive manufacturing costs. The production of standardized components is therefore dominated by large multinational companies. When it comes to systems suppliers, one purchases mainly standardized components and concentrates on the building of systems.

Even among systems suppliers, large volumes are frequently judged to be important, not least because of the rise in costs of both hardware and software development. Consequently, mergers and cooperation agreements have become quite a common feature of the telecommunications industry. The principal systems suppliers for public networks include Alcatel of France, AT&T of the USA, Ericsson of Sweden, NEC of Japan, Northern Telecom of Canada and Siemens of Germany.

Ericsson's AXE system used in public networks is based on a computerized switching technique designed for telephone stations. In order to be less affected by technological changes, Ericsson tries to modify its basic systems by replacing single components.

AXE systems frequently also serve as switches for mobile telephony networks. A complete mobile telephony network consists of two parts – one part comprises a fixed system with the related switches, base radio stations and transmission equipment and the second part is made up of mobile telephone units and related equipment. The fixed systems are normally delivered to local telephone operating companies, whereas the mobile units are sold directly to subscribers.

Ericsson's CME 20 network system is composed of three subsystems: a switching system, a base radio system, and an operating and support system. The switching system contains all the regular telephone functions, as well as additional functions such as call processing, traffic control and number analysis. The base station system manages radio communications with the mobile units. The operating and support system performs mainly network configurations, subscription administration, checks and measurements on the other subsystems.

The GSM standard for mobile telephony allows for the integration of systems from different suppliers into networks. The European companies Alcatel, Ericsson and Siemens were offering complete GSM systems back in 1993. When it comes to GSM networks in general, the following companies belong to the main systems suppliers in the world:

Ericsson (in 1995 its system was operational in 25 countries)
Siemens (21 countries)
Motorola (16 countries)
Nokia (13 countries)
Alcatel (9 countries)
Northern Telecom (3 countries)

Other important competitors in the field of mobile telephony systems are AT&T and NEC.

The supply of switching systems for private communications and other purposes, such as office use, is more fragmented. For example, in Germany in 1991 there were twenty-nine companies possessing permits to use frequencies for large subscriber exchanges (Zentralamt für Zulassungen im Fernmeldewesen, 31 March 1991). Altogether, these companies could offer seventy-four different large subscriber exchanges. Siemens's products predominated, with the company having a total of eleven permissions.

Ericsson's MD 110 is a large computerized subscriber exchange which has been developed since 1977. The system is a result of the development of the AXE system. AXE's function and software modularity, as well as the programing language and the support system used for the design and production of software, are located in MD 110. Thus the system is built around linked modules, where each module can function as an independent exchange, making it suitable for geographically spread organizations.

For a systems supplier it is important to build up long-term customer relations. This facilitates taking responsibility for wide-range communication solutions. The marketing challenge is normally constituted in offering cooperation that will last for years rather than in selling single products.

No matter which market is being penetrated, the first order in connection with the selection of a telephone switching system normally means the beginning of a long-term relationship between customer and supplier, in which the value of the follow-up orders is generally higher than that of the first contract. The first order is therefore of paramount importance to the systems supplier and is often obtained against intensive competition.

Apart from traditional competitive means such as price and technical performance, general quality and delivery terms, a systems supplier must be prepared to meet other demands. These relate to local production, technical cooperation, counter-purchase deals, credits and special financial arrangements. Such demands must be satisfied by the systems supplier independently or through participation in joint ventures.

Network operators: an overview

The deregulation of the telecommunications markets makes possible the competition between network operators. These operators can be grouped in several different ways. Ericsson provides one fruitful typology (*Annual Report* 1994):

- traditional telecom operators;
- new operators who joined the competition as a result of deregulation;
- new operators that have introduced new ways in which to confront the market;
- companies that operate specialized networks;
- companies with their bases in other industries.

The type of operator that dominates the market in the majority of countries is the traditional telecom operator. Many of the the traditional operators are the former monopolistic administrations, e.g. British Telecom (BT), AT&T, and Telia of Sweden. In 1991 the world's fifteen largest operators consisted of (*Teldok Yearbook 1994*):

NTT (Nippon Telegraph and Telephone)
DBP Telekom (Deutsche Bundes Post Telekom)
British Telecom
France Telecom
AT&T
GTE Corporation
SIP Italy
BellSouth
Nynex
Bell Atlantic

Ameritech
Pacific Telesis
US West
Telefonica de Espana
Southwestern Bell

BellSouth, Nynex, Bell Atlantic, Ameritech, Pacific Telesis, US West and Southwestern Bell have their origins in the former monopoly of AT&T in the USA. These seven regional operators dominate the US local services markets, but they are also allowed to compete in other geographical areas. The long-distance traffic on the territory of the USA is dominated by AT&T, MCI Communications and US Sprint.

In many countries the traditional operators may have to face competition from other operators in their own domestic markets, but, on the other hand, they normally have the possibility of spreading on to foreign markets. An example is given in the following:

> Since privatisation in 1984, BT has evolved from a state-owned monopoly acting mainly in the domestic market, into a customer oriented company with global ambitions working in a competitive market.
>
> (Bo Rehn, Managing Director, BT Nordic,
> *Teldok Yearbook 1994*)

The business sphere of BT embraces the design, construction, operation and management of networks and applications across the world. In 1994 BT had more than one hundred offices located in around thirty different countries, and was present in eight European countries.

In Sweden, the traditional Telia operator faces the competition of various domestic operators, such as Tele2 as regards stationary networks, and Comviq and Nordic Tel when it comes to mobile telephony. International operators, such as AT&T, BT and France Telecom, have also managed to establish themselves on the Swedish market.

In accordance with the typology presented by Ericsson, the second type of operators are those who joined the international competition at the time when the telecommunications markets were being opened up in various countries. Unisource (a joint venture of Telia, PTT Netherlands, the Swiss PTT and Telefonica of Spain) is a good example of such an operator. Airtouch, the American mobile telephony operator, is another.

Strategic alliances have become common in international traffic. Unisource is an early example of this. In 1994 Unisource also formed Uniworld in association with AT&T. Furthermore, BT acquired an interest in MCI Communications, the second largest long-distance operator in the USA. DBP Telekom, France Telekom and US Sprint, the third largest long-distance operator in the USA, have also announced their intention to create yet another conjoint operator.

Companies that have developed ways of confronting the market are another new type of operator that has recently emerged. MFS Communications in the USA may serve as an example here. This company has built its own optical fibre networks in about seventy-five large cities in different countries. The creation of fibre networks means that a new way in which to access telecommunications networks has been opened for customers. Energis of the UK – a power company – and British Rail are other good examples of this type of operator.

Companies that are already operating specialized telecommunications networks constitute the fourth operator type suggested by Ericsson's typology. Companies of this type normally also show interest in related telecommunications areas. Swift of the UK operates a network for banking services, and the Sita company specializes in networks for aviation telephony.

The fifth type of operator consists of companies that have their bases in other industries, and which are trying to expand into the area of telecommunications. Many of them have experience in network design from totally different industries. Telivo of Finland and Amsterdam Power of the Netherlands are new telecommunications operators with their roots in power supply.

The nature of the relationship between systems suppliers and network operators varies. In Australia, for example, Telecom Australia shares Ericsson's knowledge of market introduction of new services to other countries, and the two companies cooperate in marketing their services to end-users.

Another example is the close relationship between MFS Communications and Ericsson. The company has been deeply involved in the planning of MFS's expansion from the very start, providing operational support around the world wherever networks were being established.

The majority of the new operators are emerging in the mobile telephony section of the telecommunications industry. Frequently, these operators are established by banks or other financial institutions, and by international telecommunications operators. For example, in 1995 there were sixty local operators engaged in GSM networks in forty-three countries. Three operators were active in Australia and Sweden respectively. Two GSM operators competed in Denmark, Finland, France, Germany, Greece, Hong Kong, Hungary, Norway, the

Philippines, Portugal, South Africa, Thailand and the UK. One GSM operator was established in no less than twenty-eight countries.

In Sweden, Telia Mobitel is engaged in Ericsson's GSM system, Comviq operates Motorola and Siemens's systems, while Nordictel operates Nokia's system. Telia Mobitel is a subsidiary of Telia AB, the former monopoly administration. The business mission of this subsidiary company is contained in its focus on the introduction of mobile telecommunications in Sweden and the offering of services to Swedish end-users abroad (*Annual Report* 1993). At the end of 1993 Telia Mobitel had 785,000 customers, including both individual consumers and companies. Cooperation agreements had been signed with GSM operators both in and outside Europe.

The competition on the operators market is intense and there is continuous pressure for new products and services:

> Today it is more crucial to develop new products and services for a common market, not within the same technical area. Based on market segmentation we have developed a number of new products.
>
> (Seth Myrby, Managing Director, Telia Mobitel,
> *Annual Report* 1993)

The presence of strong competition is also one of the reasons for Telia Mobitel's international expansion:

> Since we took the initiative to the GSM development in the early 1980s, we have expanded our international relations. The Swedish market is limited and even though we expect increased volumes, our market shares will probably decrease. This is possible to partly compensate by rationalizations, but also by an international expansion. As a partner in company groups we build mobile telephony networks in, among other places, the Baltic region, Hungary, Italy and Russia.
>
> (Seth Myrby, Managing Director, Telia Mobitel,
> *Annual Report* 1993)

Retailers: strategic groups on the Swedish mobile telephony market

In 1995 there were three mobile telephony operators in Sweden, Telia Mobitel, Nordictel (known under the brand name of Europolitan) and Comviq GSM. Telia Mobitel is the market leader, working in close cooperation with the systems supplier Ericsson, and operating two analog NMT networks and one digital GSM network. Through the parent company, Telia Mobitel has the use of Teliabutiken's retail chain. Europolitan is a smaller operator and is responsible for the GSM network of Nokia. Europolitan distributes through Europolitan stores. Comviq GSM controls around one-third of the market, and has close relations with Siemens and Motorola.

Retailers on the Swedish market consisted originally of a number of specialists in mobile telephony, but with time a few large retail chains became dominant. Teliabutikerna, Unisource Mobile (controlling the Geab stores) and Europolitan stores are regarded as the leading chains. The expansion of the private consumer market was accompanied by the appearance of supermarkets for consumer electronics, such as Onoff and City, which are now firmly established.

Figure 4.2 illustrates strategic groups of retailers on the Swedish mobile telephony market in 1995. The groups comprised of Telia-butikerna and Unisource Mobile, and the Europolitan stores will be analysed against the background of their relations with operators.

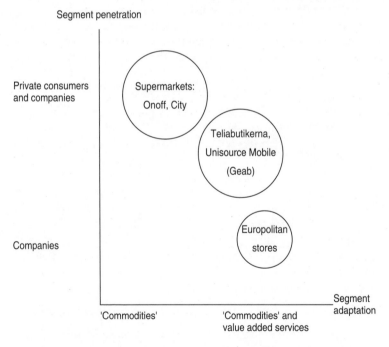

Figure 4.2 Strategic groups of retailers on the Swedish mobile telephony market, 1995

Teliabutikerna offers a wide range of telecommunications equipment, including mobile telephony from Telia Mobitel, to private consumers and companies. In 1995 this chain consisted of around one hundred stores. Although one can detect a tendency to offer the entire systems for telecommunications and computers, segment adaptation has not been established in any firm way (Tall, 1995).

Unisource Mobile is a subsidiary of Unisource NV of the Netherlands. This company is ambitious to become a leader in the area of network operations. In 1994 Unisource Mobile acquired the Swedish Geab retail chain which offers mobile telephony, telefax and computer equipment. In the middle of 1995 there were thirty-three stores, with both private consumers and companies as target groups. However, the private market segment seems to be the most interesting and a certain adaptation strategy can be discerned here:

> As the use of mobile phones spreads into the mass market, there will be a demand for new types of value-added services. A direct link to end-users will be another cornerstone of the strategy of Unisource Mobile. The first steps in this direction have already been taken by acquiring Geab, Sweden's largest chain of retail stores for mobile services and equipment, and the German service provider D-plus. This concept for service distribution will be established in several other European countries.
>
> (Unisource NV, *Annual Report* 1994, in Tall 1995)

One reason for the willingness to adapt is the growing tendency of the consumers to consider mobile telephony equipment as a commodity.

In the middle of 1995 there were eleven Europolitan stores, located primarily in the Stockholm area. This chain specializes in mobile telephony for companies. One of the reasons behind the establishment of a retail chain was to come closer to the end-users (Tall 1995). This has been necessary due to the fact that Europolitan's products are becoming increasingly sophisticated. The products and the accompanying services demand qualified sales personnel and proper customer education. Another reason is that the bargaining power of the previous retailers was too high.

End-users: companies' purchase of large subscriber exchanges

In a survey examining seventy-two Swedish companies' preferences in purchasing large subscriber exchanges, it was found that the most important factors were the terms of post-purchase services offered by the suppliers, the technical specifications of the exchanges and the possibility of receiving instructions in the use of the exchanges (Gorringe and Hartikainen 1991):

• Most important: post-purchase services offered by the suppliers.
• Very important: technical specifications of the exchanges, instructions in the use of the exchanges.
• Rather important: price, a broad product range offered by the suppliers.
• Less important: design of complementary products, financing offered by the suppliers.

The authors also conducted personal interviews with eight companies in the sample. The representatives of five of those companies (the purchasing managers responsible for the particular purchases) considered the purchasing process to be cumbersome. Some of their reasons included:

• difficulties in estimating the price and the quality of the exchanges and complementary products;
• difficulties in comparing information received from different suppliers;
• information shortage and lack of knowledge.

The eight interviews were divided into three parts, namely perception of needs, collection of information and composition of decision-making groups.

Perception of needs

Why did you need a subscriber exchange? Two of the companies had moved to new premises and increased their personnel. Three regarded their old exchanges to be so out of date that service was no longer available. Two of these companies and two others also considered their old exchanges to be technically too old-fashioned. All these companies needed better service.

The need for a new exchange was growing from within, and no representative regarded themselves as influenced by suppliers. Furthermore, none of the companies had a clear picture of the financial implications of the two options: to keep the old exchange or to buy a new one.

When did you discover that you needed a new exchange? For those companies that had finalized their purchase, the buying process, starting from the realization of the need up to the completion of the deal, took between two months and one year. The companies trying to make an evaluation of the offer expected at least a year before the deal was completed. The two companies that had recently moved to new premises took only three months to close their deals.

How long did you have your old exchange? Two companies reported that they had had their old exchanges for five to eight years, four companies used their old exchanges for about ten years, and two companies for fourteen and twenty-five years respectively.

Collection of information

What sources of information did you use in the search for a supplier? The most common way to collect information was through the supplying company's salesmen. Four companies were contacted by a salesman before they actually started searching for information themselves. In three other cases, someone in the company knew someone else employed by the supplier and established the contact.

Other sources of information included references from other buying companies, advertisements, exhibitions and seminars.

How did you evaluate the suppliers and their offers? Many companies trusted the salesman and combined the information received from him with that gathered from the representatives of other buying companies. Two companies turned to consultants or other experts.

Composition of decision-making groups

What parties were involved in the purchase of the new exchanges? In seven cases, the initiative was taken by the financial manager or another manager responsible for purchasing. In one case, the initiative came from the company's president and his management team as a whole. These managers also conducted the evaluation of the suppliers and their offers. Two companies reported that both the managers responsible for computer systems and the switchboard operators took part in the evaluation. The buying decisions were made in principle by those who took the initiative in the first place.

What important product features were put forward by the parties involved in the buying process? In addition to various views coming from the actors mentioned above, switchboard operators came up with several suggestions. They emphasized particularly the ergonomic features and showed a preference for displays that were easy to read. This group frequently regarded the technical specifications of the equipment as difficult to understand.

Purchasing managers would often prefer to keep the old exchanges and were very particular about the reliability of the equipment.

Financial managers were usually very price sensitive and would consider the ways of financing the purchases, whereas the staff responsible for computers were concerned about the communication between the exchange and other computer systems.

5

DEVELOPMENT OF INTERNATIONAL BUSINESS STRATEGIES
The Ericsson case

Following the strategy framework of the book, this chapter presents the Ericsson case as regards development of international business strategies. This in-depth study is quite comprehensive and covers a long period of time.[1] Strategy development of the group as a whole, as well as that of individual business areas, is described. The business areas of Public Telecommunications, Radio Communications and Business Communications are especially focused on, including the development of their strategies on the major markets, such as Germany, the USA and partly Japan.

The Ericsson group is recognized for its advanced systems and products for wired and mobile telecommunications used in public and private networks. The parent company, Telefonaktiebolaget LM Ericsson, and the group's headquarters are located in Stockholm, Sweden. Ericsson had about 70,000 employees in 1993 (Table 5.1) and was active in more than 100 countries.

Ericsson gives high priority to research and development, which accounted for roughly SEK 11 billion in 1993. This was equal to 17 per cent of the net sales amounting to SEK 63 billion. The total technical expenses, including costs connected with the adaptation of products to local markets, amounted in 1993 to 21 per cent of net sales.

That year the group was divided into five business areas which were globally responsible for the development and marketing of their products and systems. The business areas concerned were: Public Telecommunications (30 per cent of sales to external customers in 1993, Table 5.2), Radio Communications (41), Business Networks (earlier two areas: Business Communications and Cable and Networks) (20), Defence Systems (3) and Components (6). Major systems include the AXE switching system for public telecommunications, mobile telephony systems and the MD 110 subscriber exchange for offices and business communications.

The AXE system was operational in 105 countries in 1993, with 80 million lines installed or on order (*Annual Report* 1993). Ericsson's mobile telephone system served 13.2 million subscribers in 64 countries in the same year, with the world market share for analog systems being 40 per cent. The MD 110 subscriber exchange had a total of 7 million lines installed in 1993.

Each business area consists of a number of business elements and is globally responsible for developing and delivering its products and systems. The general manager of each business area issues instructions regarding strategies, pricing, and other topics relevant to the business elements. The business area manager is globally responsible for the operating results.

A local company is normally a subsidiary or a company for which Ericsson has management responsibility. Local companies can be engaged in sales, product development and manufacturing, with full responsibility for the operating results. In some cases a company may export part of its production.

In turn, the business areas and the local companies are supported and controlled by the Corporate Executive Committee. In 1993 the Committee was made up of the President and Chief Executive Officer (CEO) Lars Ramqvist and Carl Wilhelm Ros, Executive Vice President and Chief Financial Officer. In order to support this management team there were nine corporate staffs in 1993.

System knowledge, international experience and customer orientation were the major ingredients of the corporate strategy in the mid-1990s. For a system supplier it is important to build up long-term customer relations. This facilitates taking responsibility for total communication solutions. The marketing challenge is frequently constituted in offering cooperation that will last for years rather than in selling single products. Most of the contracts that are being signed are valid for prolonged orders, complementing the existing systems. Hence, the once installed base of, for example, the systems of AXE, the mobile telephony and MD 110 are continuously extended. In many countries long-term agreements covering prolonged deliveries are signed.

Europe dominates as a market, accounting for 56 per cent of Ericsson's sales in 1993 (Table 5.3). Other markets include the USA and Canada (12 per cent), Latin America (11 per cent), Asia (13 per cent, excluding the Middle East), Oceania (5 per cent), the Middle East (2 per cent) and Africa (1 per cent).

Table 5.1 Summary of the financial accounts of the Ericsson group, 1983–93 (SEK billion)

	1983	1984	1985	1986	1987	1988	1989	1990	1991	1992	1993
Results for the year											
Net sales	25.2	29.4	32.5	31.6	32.4	31.3	39.5	45.7	45.8	47.0	63.0
Operating income	2.5	2.3	1.7	2.3	2.2	2.7	4.6	5.7	2.3	1.8	3.5
Financial net	-0.8	-0.9	-1.0	-1.2	-0.9	-0.6	-0.4	-0.2	-0.2	-0.2	0
Income before taxes	1.8	1.6	0.9	0.9	1.1	1.8	3.7	4.9	1.6	1.3	3.1
Year-end position											
Total assets	30.6	37.6	37.1	34.2	33.3	34.6	40.9	47.2	49.6	56.1	67.5
Working capital	12.8	17.0	16.7	14.7	13.9	12.9	15.0	17.0	17.5	20.1	20.9
Long-term liabilities	6.7	7.7	8.6	11.1	10.9	9.9	9.0	8.8	11.0	12.6	14.5
Stockholders equity[1]	8.6	9.3	9.5	9.7	11.5	12.4	14.7	17.4	17.4	18.1	23.5
Backlog of orders	21.6	25.1	23.1	23.6	24.2	26.9	29.4	30.4	28.8	38.0	45.3
No. of employees, thousands											
Worldwide	70.8	75.1	78.2	72.6	70.9	65.1	69.2	70.2	71.2	66.2	69.6
Sweden	34.5	37.5	40.2	38.6	37.4	32.1	32.2	30.8	31.2	30.0	31.8
Other information											
Depreciation	0.9	1.0	1.3	1.1	1.2	1.0	1.3	1.6	1.9	2.2	2.6
Research & development											
expenses	2.0	2.4	2.8	3.1	3.2	3.5	4.3	4.9	7.0	7.4	10.9
% of sales	7.8	8.0	8.6	9.9	9.9	11.3	10.9	10.7	15.4	15.7	17.4
Ratios											
Return on equity, %	10.9	8.5	6.1	6.9	7.5	11.5	17.5	20.4	5.3	2.8	14.5
Return on capital employed, %	17.8	13.6	11.3	13.1	13.1	16.0	23.7	25.9	12.1	9.9	12.9
Debt/equity ratio	1.1	1.5	1.5	1.1	1.0	0.8	0.6	0.5	0.7	0.8	0.7

Source: Annual Reports
Note: 1 After full conversion

Table 5.2 Summary of Ericsson's sales to external customers by business area, 1983–93 (%)

Business areas	Years										
	1983	1984	1985	1986	1987	1988	1989	1990	1991	1992	1993
Public telecommunications	34	33	32	33	34	44	44	45	43	35	30
Radio communications	6	7	7	9	9	16	20	25	27	32	41
Business communications[1,3]	28	31	31	29	28	12	13	11	10	13	20
Cable and networks[3]	14	13	13	11	10	9	13	14	14	14	—
Defence systems	6	6	7	9	10	8	8	4	4	4	3
Components	3	3	3	2	2	2	2	1	2	2	6
Networks[2]	9	7	7	7	7	10	—	—	—	—	—

Source: Annual Reports
Notes:
1 Information Systems until 1987
2 Joined Cables in 1989
3 Business Networks in 1993

Table 5.3 Summary of Ericsson's sales to geographic regions, 1983–93 (%)

Geographic regions	Years										
	1983	1984	1985	1986	1987	1988	1989	1990	1991	1992	1993
Europe, excl. Sweden	34	35	38	43	49	49	48	47	44	47	46
Sweden	19	21	20	22	23	19	16	12	13	13	10
USA and Canada	11	12	10	10	8	7	10	13	13	12	12
Latin America	12	12	13	10	8	10	9	12	13	11	11
Asia, excl. Middle East	4	6	8	5	3	4	6	6	8	9	13
Oceania, Australia, New Zealand	5	4	5	5	5	6	6	5	4	4	5
Middle East	11	7	4	3	2	3	3	3	4	3	2
Africa	4	3	2	2	2	2	2	2	1	1	1

Source: Annual Reports

For different reasons, Germany has become an increasingly interesting market for Ericsson. In the late 1980s the strategic importance of the German market was clearly perceivable, and success in that country was considered crucial for Ericsson's continued expansion in Europe. In his first yearly review the new CEO, Lars Ramqvist, announced in the *Annual Report* of 1990 that the business area of Public Telecommunications had broken into new geographical markets, including Germany. Furthermore, in the same year two German subsidiaries were established (Ericsson Mobilfunk GmbH and Ericsson Eurolab GmbH) with growing expectations for the AXE system to be introduced on to the German market.

All business areas of the Ericsson group had earlier included separate subsidiaries in Germany. In 1993–4 these were consolidated into one company, Ericsson Deutschland GmbH, located in Düsseldorf. The company is organized along customer-oriented 'divisions' for Mannesmann (mobile telephony systems and equipment), Deutsche Telekom (public telecommunications and mobile telephony), private customers (primarily switching systems for offices) and mobile telephones. A common development unit is also present.

The importance of an active presence in the USA was explicitly formulated by Ericsson's corporate management in the early 1980s. This country was regarded as very interesting, both as a new market for the group's products and as a source of knowledge (CEO Björn Svedberg, *Annual Report* 1984). Thus, in the early 1980s Ericsson started to give priority to the huge and relatively well-developed market for information technology in the USA. (Information technology means transmission and handling of voice, data, image and text in public and private networks for communications.) In previous years Ericsson was not extensively represented in the USA, which was primarily due to the monopoly of American Telephone and Telegraph (AT&T) in the telecommunications area.

The market volume was not the only factor that had turned the USA into a very important market strategically for Ericsson as well as its competitors. Another reason was that the deregulation process supported by the governments involved had gone further in that country compared to many others. The USA was therefore regarded as a very important reference market and as a source of experience in dealing with the coming deregulations of other markets. In addition, it abounded in both customers and competitors. In an early phase this is how the CEO motivated the focus on the USA market:

Our plans also demand that we acquire a strong position in the U.S.A. We regard this as crucial in order to become an active partner in the information systems industry during the 1990's. The U.S. will then doubtlessly be the leading market in information technology. This country already is the primary source of new technology and new marketing ideas.

(CEO Björn Svedberg, *Annual Report* 1983)

Some years later the CEO was asked if the US market was of crucial importance to Ericsson's corporate strategy in the 1990s:

In fact, the U.S. is not decisive in terms of production volume. But the market is quite important, considering that the development of the service sector has gone further compared to Europe's service sector. This means that we can place product development projects in the U.S., which might be of use to us on other markets.

(CEO Björn Svedberg, *Veckans Affärer* 1988)

Due to the deregulation process in telecommunications, Japan has also become accessible to Ericsson. The CEO, Lars Ramqvist, regarded this market in the early 1990s (*Affärsvärlden* 1992) as one of the most promising and important telecommunications markets in the world. When it comes to Japan, the strategy description in this chapter discusses Ericsson's activities primarily with regard to the mobile telephony market.

STRATEGIC DEVELOPMENT OF THE ERICSSON GROUP AND THE CORPORATE STRATEGY IN THE MID-1990s

The Ericsson group was originally started by two Swedish pioneers in 1876 in order to exploit the new communication technology. On the occasion of LM Ericsson's centenary in 1976, three books (Attman *et al.* 1977a,b,c) appeared describing the main lines of strategic development during the 'first hundred years'. In one of them, Marcus Wallenberg Jr, who took an active part in the reconstruction of LM Ericsson after the Kreuger crash in 1932, is described as one of the most prominent figures of the Ericsson group and the parent company. He became Vice Chairman of the Board in 1933 and since then has played a major role, influencing the company's policies in the capacity of Chairman and then Honorary Chairman until 1982. In the Introduction to the books he states:

With his invention of the telephone in 1876, Alexander Grahamn Bell had created an instrument that solved the problem of fast, direct communications to serve a rapidly expanding industrialized society. The new instrument permitted direct contact between persons remote from each other, something that had not been possible up to that time.

The telephone became the foundation of a worldwide industry, within which Swedish enterprise gained a leading position. For this, we have to thank two Swedish pioneers, Lars Magnus Ericsson and Henrik Tore Cedergren. Each perceived at an early stage the importance of the new communications medium, sensing its growth potential and the role it was to play in the increasingly rapid transformation of society. They were men with strong faith in the future, matched by confidence in their own capability.

Lars Magnus Ericsson, a farmer's son from Värmland County in Middle Sweden, had been forced to make his way in the world at an early age; in the process, he had acquired a solid base of practical experience. When the telephone was introduced in Sweden in 1877, the year after he started his workshop in Stockholm under the name of LM Ericsson & Co., he had an opportunity to study the invention closely. He began to make telephone instruments and developed his own new designs. Within the space of a few years, the Company's production was concentrated on the manufacture of telephone equipment.

H. T. Cedergren, who had a technological training, clearly appreciated the practical applications of the new communications medium. He therefore reacted strongly against the high tariffs set by the Bell Company and its Swedish subsidiary. In 1883, with the expressed purpose of providing inexpensive telephone service to every household in the country, Cedergren formed Stockholms Allmänna Telefonaktiebolag. The company was successful and by 1885, Stockholm had the highest telephone density in the world.

Comparable growth occurred in cities in Sweden's provinces, where local telephone associations were formed. These associations ordered equipment from LM Ericsson. The company's largest customers were, however, Stockholms Allmänna Telefonaktiebolag and Telegrafverket, the national board of telegraphs. With time, both customers established their own factories which competed with LM Ericsson. Parallel with its early success in Sweden, the company set its sights on exports. From the 1890's on, foreign markets were completely dominant and manufacturing subsidiaries were established in several European countries.

Cedergren had founded Svensk-Dansk-Ryska Telefon AB with the support of K. A. and Marcus Wallenberg Sr., of Stockholms Enskilda Bank, and I. Glückstadt of Den Danske Landmandsbank. Subsequently, he had an opportunity to develop in foreign countries the telephone operating experience he had gained in Sweden. He was successful. The telephone concessions in Moscow and Warsaw were won against severe competition. The same pioneering spirit lay behind the acquisition of the concession in Mexico.

The various forms of co-operation and competition that had developed between the two pioneering Swedish companies led in 1918 to their merger under the name Allmänna Telefonaktiebolaget LM Ericsson – abbreviated to Telefonaktiebolaget LM Ericsson after a few years. The merger had hardly come into effect, however, before the company suffered a succession of reverses. The earlier successful investments in Russia – with factories in Leningrad, and telephone exchanges and a telephone network in Moscow – were lost as a result of the revolution. When it became clear that the company would receive no compensation, the share capital had to be written down by fifty per cent to cover part of the losses.

The situation was complicated by the fact that the company, which had been successful in manual telephony, had fallen behind technically by not having invested in automatic exchanges early enough. Once a system for automatic telephony had been developed in the 1920's, the company concentrated on winning telephone concessions in various countries with the objective of capturing new markets by utilizing the telephone operating experience of the Cedergren enterprises.

Large capital resources were required, however, and it was in this context that LM Ericsson's management began to co-operate with Ivar Kreuger, who made the company a part of his sphere of interest. Company funds – some acquired through loans of new issues of shares – were transferred to other parts of the Kreuger Group whose operations were alien to Ericsson's. The company's liquidity was undermined at the same time as the concessions required large injections of capital. A shareholding representing a majority interest in LM Ericsson was sold by Kreuger to the company's toughest competitor, International Telephone & Telegraph

Corporation (ITT), in the United States. The Kreuger crash in 1932 placed LM Ericsson in a catastrophic situation. The company's very survival was at stake.

Long and difficult negotiations, supported by the Swedish authorities and banks, created a basis for LM Ericsson's continued operations. The company was to function as an independent Swedish enterprise and ITT's voting rights on the Ericsson board were restricted to roughly one-third of the total. The company's debts were consolidated and the necessary operating capital was made available through the Swedish banks.

An extensive program was undertaken to rationalize and economize. Substantial consolidation was effected in all areas of the company's operations. The work of reconstruction extended into the beginning of the 1940's, by which time the after-effects of the crash and the depression had been overcome. The company had recovered its stability. During the remaining years of the war its financial position was further strengthened.

When the postwar period opened up new opportunities in the international market, LM Ericsson was financially and technically equipped to take the initiatives that have positioned the company in the foremost ranks among the world's telecommunications manufacturers. Technical and administrative skills created sales successes that gave LM Ericsson an increasingly international character, with sales and manufacturing companies in many countries.

ITT sold its holdings in 1960 and the shares were placed primarily with the investing public in Sweden and, to a lesser degree, in other European markets. LM Ericsson thereby regained its independent Swedish character. A world enterprise had been built.

(Marcus Wallenberg Jr, Honorary Chairman of the Board of
LM Ericsson, Attman *et al.* 1977a)

The general strategy in dealing with product development from the very beginnings of LM Ericsson has been to develop products and concepts related to basic telephone technology. This has always been a common core of the group.

At the end of the 1960s a search was started for a new telephone technology in order to replace the electromechanical systems. In connection with this, in 1972 an important decision was made to start development of the so-called AXE system at the laboratories of the Ellemtel subsidiary. This system is based on the electronic computerized switching technique for telephone stations and on the use of digital networks.

In order to reduce the production capacity of electromechanical systems, a short-term adaptation had to be performed in connection with the falling demand. Meanwhile a long-term oriented adaptation for the production of electronic switching systems had to be made to meet the expected increase in demand.

Electronic technology is based on integrated circuits requiring large volumes in order to achieve competitive manufacturing costs. Hence, production of standardized components is now dominated by large American and Asian producers. When it comes to Ericsson, one purchases mainly standardized components and concentrates on the building of systems.

However, technology life cycles are becoming shorter and shorter, while development costs are getting higher and higher. An early example from a competitor:

> In the 1960's ITT had to spend about 40 million USD for developing their Pentaconda telephone switching system, with a 20 year expected life-span. Today they have to spend almost 20 times as much on System 12, with a presumed life-span of six years.
> (*Veckans Affärer* 1983a)

A consequence of the rise in costs of both hardware and software development is that larger and more standardized production volumes are desirable. In order to be less affected by the shorter technology life cycles, Ericsson tries to modify the basic systems by replacing single components.

In the Annual Report of 1982, the CEO Björn Svedberg stressed the importance of keeping the long-term perspective with regard to the group's actions. This was then, and still is, necessary for different reasons. One reason was the fact that electronics had become dominant in the main product groups. The relatively low return on capital at that time could be explained to a large extent by the adherence to the long-term perspective principle. As the CEO Björn Svedberg said: 'Eventually short-term actions for increasing profitability will not counter-balance the risk of losing a technical position' (*Annual Report* 1982).

Maintaining a strong technical position was a major argument for the estimated revenues in 1987: SEK 40 billion, as compared to SEK 20 billion in 1982. An additional objective was to double the internal financing. To finance the expansion, an objective of 14 per cent on return on total capital was set.

Ericsson's world market share as regards public telephone stations grew during the 1970s from 10 per cent to 15 per cent. The commercial results of the AXE system were considered to be the foundation of the technical development in areas related to the telecommunication area, especially the office automation area and later also mobile telephony.

MD 110, a computerized telephone switching system for offices that has been developed since 1977, was a result of the AXE system and was looked upon as the technological key to the office automation market. AXE's function and software modularity, as well as the programing language and the support system used for the design and the production of software, are located in MD 110. The system makes communication within an organization possible as regards both voice and data. MD 110 is built around linked modules, where each module can function as an independent exchange. This makes the system suitable for geographically widely spread organizations such as universities and large companies.

A somewhat amended strategy, mainly in terms of the creation of an organization for the office automation market, coupled with increased efforts on the US market, was supported in 1981 by the transformation of 'the parent company LM Ericsson with subsidiaries' to 'the Ericsson group'. A major organizational change was thus initiated.

The introduction of the business area structure was motivated to a large extent by the growing attention of the group according to strategic planning and by the desired decentralization of the operational responsibility. Even though many products required different treatment in terms of, for example, marketing, the basic technological foundation of the group still existed. The group came to be regarded as an industrial unit with synergistic advantages in research and development, production, marketing and financing.

Due mostly to internal problems, Ericsson's organization concerning the office automation market was reduced step by step in the middle of the 1980s. The historical concentration strategy became again the main priority, and when the new CEO Lars Ramqvist was appointed he expressed his concern to keep the focus on telecommunications:

> Today Ericsson has a world leading position in the telecommunications area. As we intend to keep this position, we further go for research and development. At the same time the costs of the adaptation of our products to market requirements are heavily increasing.
>
> (CEO Lars Ramqvist, *Annual Report* 1990)

Although in the early 1990s the market was characterized by restraint as a consequence of the international recession, Ericsson continued investing large sums of money in technical development:

> Looking back at the past year, I am indeed pleased to note that our strategy was correct and that our undiminished investments in technology were necessary. Without comprehensive new development programs, we would not have been able to report such strong order bookings.
>
> (CEO Lars Ramqvist, *Annual Report* 1992)

Large volumes are important if one is to develop systems and products that are to be competitive for a long time. This is one reason why mergers and cooperation agreements have become common in the telecommunications and dataprocessing industry:

> Ericsson is strong enough to be able to continue as an independent company with its own core products. We shall become even better in areas where we have our real strengths. At the same time, we must realize that we cannot do everything ourselves. Through cooperation in various areas, we are achieving efficiency and the volumes of business required to support continued development work.
>
> (CEO Björn Svedberg, *Annual Report* 1986)

Boundaries within the telecommunications area are continuously disappearing. Public networks are able to provide services which were earlier provided only by private systems. At the same time private exchanges serving the offices of various companies and organizations are becoming more efficient in linking together geographically widely spread units. This makes the division between the areas of public and private telecommunications less clear, and applies likewise to the division between stationary communication systems using cables and those using radios.

For a long time it has been possible to complement the old telephony technique with the transmission of text, data and image. But these complementary methods made up an insignificant part of the traffic in networks until the late 1980s. After that the various methods of complementation started growing, especially in the industrialized countries. This means that industrialized countries represent the fastest growing part of the telecommunications world market.

> We have not allowed the weak financial results of the last years to influence our efforts in research and development. The AXE

technology is competitive and our mobile telephony systems hold their share of the world market. The MD 110 office exchange is often recognized as one of the best systems as regards integrated handling of voice and data.

The possession of advanced technology, and of the products and systems of high quality is very important but it is not sufficient today. It is equally important to gain a strong position on the most important markets, not only by attaining volumes but also by meeting customer requirements.

Simultaneous efforts on large and important markets are certainly arduous in the short term, but it gives a strength to compete on these markets as well.

(CEO Björn Svedberg, *Annual Report* 1987)

The efforts to concentrate on systems were further intensified in 1988. This means that public telecommunications, business communications and mobile telephony systems were the ones in focus. 'One explanation of our success in mobile telephony is that we control the whole chain: AXE constitutes the system's exchange, we have radio base stations and telephones' (CEO Björn Svedberg, *Annual Report* 1988).

From 1990 combined operating results concerning the following business areas were reflected in the Annual Report under the heading Telecommunications Systems: Public Telecommunications, Radio Communications, Business Communications and Components. All operations in these areas are interrelated to a large extent, which is why the combination of their results was supposed to give a more accurate picture of the income trend for these businesses:

	(SEK million)					
	Sales			*Operating income*		
	1990	*1991*	*1992*	*1990*	*1991*	*1992*
Telecommunication systems	37,348	37,498	38,681	5,020	1,963	974

Telecommunication systems reported lower income from operations in 1992. The decrease was attributable primarily to operations on the Spanish and Mexican markets for public telecommunications. Improved operating income in public telecommunications was reported mainly from the Brazilian market. There was a substantial improvement of income from operations in the field of mobile telephone systems, whereas operating income from the mobile telephone instrument business declined, due to high costs connected with the introduction of new products. Operations in Business Communications, notably the MD 110 system, showed a sharp improvement of income (*Annual Report* 1992).

In addition to the primary focus on systems, Ericsson was also trying to build up activities on various important geographical markets. Generally, two opposite ways of describing foreign establishments of Ericsson's can be identified:

Either we first get an order and then build up resources (like in England and France), or we first build up resources and then prepare ourselves to receive orders (like in the U.S.A.). The problem of the former way is what to do if an unusually large order comes early. For many reasons large orders require local units, which takes time to organize and build up.

(Olav Hamstad, Market Coordination,
Ericsson Telecom, 25 February 1991)

A three-step approach is highlighted by the following citation:

There are three steps in our coordination of group activities. First we establish stable customer relations in individual countries. Thereafter we identify target groups for products or product groups in a number of countries. In this phase activities within more than one business area can be coordinated. Thirdly, there is a possibility to join the global activities of Ericsson Telecom.

(Heinrich Thanscheidt, Ericsson Business Communications in
Germany, 27 May 1991)

The process of getting established on the US market will be described briefly as follows. Before 1980 Ericsson was primarily represented in the USA by a sales company. A serious effort was initiated in 1980 when Ericsson and the American Atlantic Richfield company formed a common company (Anaconda-Ericsson, Inc.) based on equal shares. Atlantic Richfield contributed mainly with its cable factories. In addition, in the new company there was a channel for information technology, since Anaconda was manufacturing a small private branch exchange. Even though at that time Ericsson did not explicitly express their intentions, a clear strategy was to be established on the US information technology market. The cable activities were supposed to generate profits that were to be invested in the communications area. However, the cable activities did not prove as strong and profitable as had been expected and were therefore gradually divested.

In order to facilitate the American undertaking, the corporate management of Ericsson decided to effect an issue of shares in New York. One reason behind this decision was the fact that the Ericsson share was the most popular Swedish share on the American Stock Exchange in 1982. Thus, in the summer of 1983 Ericsson entered the New York Stock Exchange. The previous indecision regarding the issue of shares was due, among other things, to the relatively tough accounting rules. The New York Stock Exchange requires information about the turnover and financial results of each separate division and business area, which Ericsson was previously unable to produce.

The financial manager of that time responsible for these tasks described the background to the issue of shares:

> In the long run we will enter the U.S. market. Perhaps that opportunity will disappear though if we do not act immediately. And if we decide to go public on the American stock exchange, then the amount of capital has to be large.
>
> (Fritz Staffas, *Veckans Affärer* 1983b)

The issue of shares served three primary purposes. First, the company's solidity had been relatively low and this was the way to strengthen its capital base. Second, it served the purpose of getting into the American market with the products of the group. This kind of investment demands a lot of capital, that can be only found abroad. Third, presence on the Stock Exchange would probably mean exposure to a wide audience. The CEO presented the way of entering the US market:

> We are now trying to build up our market in the U.S. We have signed important cooperation agreements in order to adapt our products and systems to the requirements of that market. During 1984 we will be actively marketing our exchange for information handling, MD 110. At the same time we shall be introducing the AXE system on the market opening up to us as a result of the deregulation process.
>
> (CEO Björn Svedberg, *Annual Report* 1983)

However, the efforts invested in the US market were slow in paying off. The group's quarterly financial report from November 1984 actually showed a loss. The reasons that were put forward included:

- delays in development projects;
- component shortages;

119

- production disturbances;
- unsatisfactory invoicing in the USA.

These initial difficulties did not prevent Ericsson from pursuing the American strategy which had assumed with time a more explicit character. The objectives of the entire group were thus set to reach a considerably higher short-term profitability and to attain (*Annual Report* 1984):

- A consolidated position as one of the world's leading suppliers as regards switching systems for public networks.
- A strong position, based on the telecommunications and systems building know-how, in the information systems area (the market that emerges when telecommunications, distributed data handling and office automation will be integrated).
- A presence in the USA, a country of great importance to Ericsson both as a market and as a source of technology and knowledge.

These objectives required the putting in of large resources during the coming years.

In 1985 Ericsson purchased Atlantic Richfield's share of the common Ericsson Inc. company, which became a wholly owned subsidiary. The next year Peter Thomas was appointed as president of this company, which led to further strategy development. An ambition was to concentrate on fewer distribution channels and some key products: public telephone exchanges, office exchanges, banking terminals, mobile telephones and cables. The coordination of activities was to be performed at the headquarters in Richardson, Dallas.

Corporate management of Ericsson regards cooperation with other companies as important for the future; this is also true for quality efforts and improvement of performance of the systems and products:

> I am aware that our competitors are also continually improving their operations. At the same time, I know that within Ericsson we will continue with even more perseverance to sharply improve the price/performance of our products, and that we will continue to focus on further improving our customer relations.
>
> (CEO Lars Ramqvist, *Annual Report* 1994)

A goal of Ericsson is to become one of the handful of suppliers who will dominate the telecommunications market in coming decades (*Annual Report* 1994). The critical factors will be not only the ability to meet the technical challenges that the future offers, but to an equally high degree how successful Ericsson is in its relations with customers.

The telecom operators of the future will be entirely different from the customers with whom Ericsson has dealt earlier. It is expected that tomorrow's customer on a deregulated market will demand much closer cooperation. Regardless of the operator category, Ericsson aims at determining what each one requires in order to succeed in its efforts to sell its services to end-users. Once the requirements have been established, it is a matter of having the capability to develop technical and financial solutions.

Deregulation is creating opportunities for many new operators. At the same time Ericsson supposes that a small number of large operators will control an increasingly greater portion of the market. Thus, Ericsson wants to establish long-term relations with operators in different categories, especially with large operators.

ERICSSON'S DIVERGENCE ON THE INTERNATIONAL PUBLIC TELECOMMUNICATIONS MARKET

The computerized AXE switching system was introduced on the market in 1975. The system was judged to be the most competitive one by the public telephone administrations of Australia and France, who ordered it shortly after its market introduction. Some years later a rather large order was received from Saudi Arabia. Since then a large number of telephone administrations have chosen the AXE system as their basic telephone system.

Deregulation on national markets for telecommunications has had a decisive impact on the strategic development of Ericsson:

> Deregulations put a stop to the dominance of national public telecommunications administration, and the liberalization creates new markets for us.
>
> (Olav Hamstad, Market Coordination, Ericsson Telecom,
> 25 February 1991)

As a result of the deregulation and privatization of the telecommunications markets in many countries, there are increasing demands on flexibility and the ability rapidly to introduce new services into networks. Ericsson is therefore trying to concentrate on the enhancement of the AXE system in order to increase its capacity. This is being done with the help of such new applications as, for example, ISDN and IN (intelligent networks). The flexibility of the AXE system has been demonstrated by the fact of comprehensive orders on AXE to serve as exchanges for mobile telephony networks. The ability of quick implementation of new technology is of great importance in maintaining the competitiveness of the AXE system.

The prerequisites for continuous system development were established by selecting a modular and flexible system structure easily adaptable to new requirements (*Annual Report* 1983). The objective was to introduce new functions and increase the potential range of services in already installed networks.

Tables 5.4 and 5.5 give financial statistics and statistics on sales for various geographic regions in the Public Telecommunications business area. In 1993, 8.7 million local lines and 3 million transit lines of AXE were installed (the telephone of an individual subscriber is connected to a local station which is linked in turn to other stations). The system in that year was installed in 105 countries with 80 million lines installed and on order (*Annual Report* 1993).

The Public Telecommunications business area has production facilities in subsidiaries or associated companies in about fifteen countries throughout the world. In addition to the AXE system, the business area's programme includes products covering telex, data processing and transmission equipment.

As a result of the weak market, the declining exchange rate for the US dollar and the continued large development investments necessary for the adaptation of AXE to market requirements in the USA (and UK), the business area's income for 1986 was unsatisfactory. A rationalization programme including reorganization and adjustment of overhead costs to current market conditions was therefore initiated. The programme, covering the years between 1986 and 1988, involved a reduction of a total of 2,800 jobs, for instance.

Table 5.4 Summary of financial information of the Public Telecommunications business area of Ericsson, 1983–90 (SEK billion)

	Years							
	1983	1984	1985	1986	1987	1988	1989	1990
Net sales, external	8.5	9.7	10.6	10.3	10.9	13.7	17.3	20.4
Order bookings, external	8.8	10.8	11.1	10.3	11.7	15.9	17.4	21.6
Operating income, after depreciation	1.6	1.9	1.3	1.2	1.3	1.9	3.5	3.8

Source: Annual Reports

Table 5.5 Summary of Ericsson's Public Telecommunications sales to geographic regions, 1983–93 (%)

Geographic regions	Years										
	1983	1984	1985	1986	1987	1988	1989	1990	1991	1992	1993
Europe, excl. Sweden	33	30	29	35	53	59	59	61	50	49	50
Sweden	5	6	10	16	9	7	6	5	8	8	6
USA and Canada	8	8	5	5	3	1	1	2	5	5	4
Latin America	20	21	21	19	18	16	15	16	18	19	19
Asia	20	23	23	12	7	6	10	6	12	11	14
Oceania, Australia, New Zealand	7	7	9	9	8	7	6	7	5	6	5
Africa	7	5	3	4	2	4	3	3	2	2	2

Source: Annual Reports

As was also the case in the previous year, in 1988 the largest orders for AXE came from industrialized countries, which further underscored the importance of investments on these markets.

Figure 5.1 summarizes the strategic development of telephone exchanges of the Public Telecommunications business area of Ericsson between 1975 and 1993. The implemented strategy reflects the character of geographic divergence, showing that markets in Europe and other parts of the industrialized world have become increasingly important. Here, companies and organizations demand more professional services and larger volumes. Special efforts have been made to penetrate further the markets on which the AXE system is already established and to enter new markets (*Annual Report* 1987). Deregulation in the USA and Germany has enabled both Ericsson and other competitors to enter these markets. The processes involved in entry will be illustrated by the example of Ericsson, showing how the implementation of the divergence strategy works in more detail.

Ericsson on the German public telecommunications market

Deutsche Bundespost Telekom selected in 1990 the Flexnode consortium as one of three suppliers of cross-connect (transmission) equipment for the German telecommunications network. Ericsson was one of three members of the consortium. The order was regarded as strategically important for Ericsson's growth in the field of public telecommunications in Germany (*Annual Report* 1990). Furthermore, in 1992 Ericsson received a breakthrough order for a broadband system to be used by Deutsche Bundespost Telekom in a pilot network.

The former West Germany was traditionally a closed market which Ericsson was unable to penetrate (even though the business area of Ericsson Information Systems established sales activities in Düsseldorf in the early 1980s). As the global deregulation process reached this country, Ericsson's management perceived an opportunity:

> West Germany was earlier a blind spot on the world map of Ericsson. When Deutsche Telekom announced deregulation we became very interested and decided to start penetrating this market. This also applied to the former East Germany and its five regions.
> (Olav Hamstad, Market Coordination, Ericsson Telecom, 25 February 1991)

As a result of the deregulation process, Deutsche Bundespost has been divided into three sectors, including Deutsche Bundespost Telekom

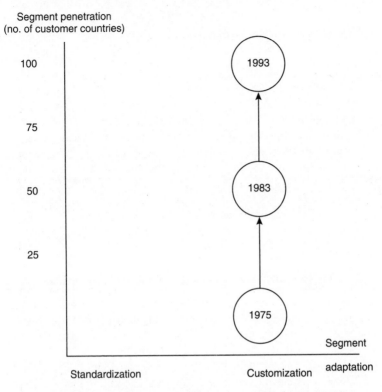

Figure 5.1 Strategic divergence of telephone exchanges of the Public Telecommunications business area of Ericsson, 1975–93

AG. Deutsche Telekom makes decisions as regards the technical requirements for the country. It also approves products and assigns radio frequencies for different communications products. 'Germany is officially an open market, but this is not true in reality.

> Those who want to compete have to adapt to the technical requirements of Deutsche Telekom, and not to the needs of the customers.
> (Heinrich Thanscheidt, Ericsson Business Communications in Germany, 27 May 1991)

When Ericsson Telecom decided to penetrate the German market on a large scale, one of the first steps was to establish a company that would develop products for the entire European market. The company

125

called Ericsson Eurolab Deutschland GmbH was established in 1990 and located in Aachen, Germany.

In the early 1990s Ericsson Telecom was considering cooperation with a large industrial company in Germany:

> We were aware of the persistence required for achieving success in Germany. Therefore, we thought that we needed an established and well-reputed partner. The first two measures were thus to spread our name on the market through a comprehensive advertising campaign, and to search for candidates for a partnership. Our shares of the market have grown rapidly, however, during the last years. This means that we are now more doubtful about a partnership.
>
> (Olav Hamstad, Market Coordination, Ericsson Telecom, 25 February 1991)

Ericsson on the US public telecommunications market

Ericsson's activities in the USA were rather limited until the early 1970s. At that time, Ericsson owned a part of the American telecommunication company Northern Electric, and the public AKE exchange (a precursor of the AXE exchange) was sold by Northern Electric of the USA.

When competition was gradually being allowed at the end of the decade, the American telecommunications market became attractive to new private companies. MCI Communications Corporation was the first new company to establish itself in the area of long-distance traffic.

> There was an intensive debate on competition in the U.S. Many people meant that new companies should only choose profitable lines and that no one should bother about thinly populated areas.
>
> (Dick Ryberg, former North America operations, Ericsson Telecom, 17 February 1994)

Ericsson delivered relatively extensive volumes of customized analog transmission equipment primarily to MCI. Later some AXE systems were also delivered. This meant that technological customization had been initiated for the first American customer.

In 1981–2 the management of Ericsson Radio Systems was engaged in a serious effort to launch mobile telephony systems on the US market. As these rely on AXE systems, joining forces with Public Telecommunications was a natural step. (The two had had previous experience of deliveries to the Scandinavian NMT network for mobile telephony.) In this way Ericsson started offering systems for mobile telephony, including AXE, on the American market in early 1982.

> We soon realized that extensive local presence was necessary to become an attractive long-term supplier in the U.S.A. We had to show the market that we were there to stay.
>
> (Dick Ryberg, former North America operations, Ericsson Telecom, 17 February 1994)

Experience gained from the business discussions with, among others, MCI and various potential buyers of the mobile telephony systems from Ericsson, resulted in the management starting to consider a large-scale establishment on the American market in the early 1980s. After further investigations and discussions, the activities of Public Telecommunications were placed in Dallas, Texas.

> Ove Ericsson, the responsible manager for the business area, told us that we were going to do something that we hadn't done before. First, we would build up resources and then wait for business deals, and not the other way round, as we are used to do.
>
> (Dick Ryberg, former North America operations, Ericsson Telecom, 17 February 1994)

Thus, the programme initiated in the USA was regarded as being of major importance to the business area of Public Telecommunications (*Annual Report* 1984). The resources that were being built up were long-term investments for the future which would not immediately contribute to improvements in the earnings or return on the capital employed. Nor was the programme of such a scope that it would jeopardize the opportunities for strong programmes in other markets.

At the end of 1982 the first Dallas unit consisted of ten designers, a few installation engineers, some technical assistants in charge of support and maintenance, and a few administrators. At the end of 1984 more than 200 programers and engineers were employed at the emerging research, development and support centre in Dallas. As in previous years, however, sales of the Public Telecommunications business area on the US market consisted in 1984 mainly of transmission equipment delivered to independent 'common carriers' handling long-distance traffic.

At the end of 1983 some restructuring of telecommunications operations in the USA was initiated, whereby the seven regional Bell operating companies (Ameritech, Bell Atlantic, Bell South, Nynex,

Pacific Telesis, Southwestern Bell and US West) were divested from AT&T. These companies could then choose their own suppliers of telephone exchange equipment. The Canadian Northern Telecom company and Western Electric (earlier the production unit of AT&T) continued receiving orders from the Bell companies, just as before. The orders concerned, for instance, local stations for long-distance traffic.

On the US market for local stations there were initially six competitors: Alcatel from France, Ericsson, NEC from Japan, Northern Telecom, Siemens from Germany and AT&T. Alcatel and NEC left the market rather early. Even though Ericsson concentrated on the seven regional Bell companies, it was aware that a large number of other potential customers existed:

> The Bells are very demanding and they are the most interesting customers for us. I think there are over one thousand telecommunication operators, besides the seven Bells.
>
> (Dick Ryberg, former North America operations, Ericsson Telecom, 17 February 1994)

The strategy concerning the Public Telecommunications business area in the USA was developing according to the original plan (*Annual Report* 1986). The Bell companies analysed and evaluated the AXE system through the control organization Bellcore (Bell Communications Research). The first phase brought orders of AXE stations for field tests from Nynex in New York and US West in Canon City, Colorado. AXE equipment was also delivered to Southwestern Bell in Dallas and Houston in order to be tested on the market.

The first AXE station was put into operation in Canon City in 1987. After that US West ordered AXE to replace the older electromechanical stations in Idaho. Southwestern Bell, Bell South and Nynex followed with orders of AXE in various designs, meaning that business relations had been established with four out of the seven Bell companies (*Annual Report* 1987). Ericsson's objective was 'to attain 10% of the local stations market in the U.S. in the early 1990's' (*Veckans Affärer*, 1988). This corresponded to approximately 700,000 lines per year.

However, development on the US market in 1988 did not happen quickly. The speed of replacements of the older telephone stations was slow, and demand was lower than the previous year.

> Despite our investigations and market plans, including market share goals, I think that we were over-optimistic when it comes to

market prices and that we under-estimated costs of technological adaptation to the American market.

(Dick Ryberg, former North America operations, Ericsson
Telecom, 17 February 1994)

In 1989 Ericsson signed contracts for deliveries of local stations to three Bell companies. Reaching the status of a 'third supplier' to Southwestern Bell, US West and Nynex was seen as a promise of further offers to come (*Annual Report* 1989). When it comes to the number of installed telephone lines, all the seven Bell companies belong to the fifteen largest public telecommunication operators in the world.

In 1990, volume orders and general agreements were signed in the USA and around 400,000 lines were installed: 'A good base has been established for gaining a 10% share of the market for local exchanges in 1991, which was the initial target of Ericsson's program for the U.S.' (*Annual Report* 1990).

AXE sales increased during 1991 and a total of 700,000 lines had been installed, mainly for the two operators, US West and South-western Bell. Equipment for nearly one million local and trunk lines was delivered in 1992 to upgrade AXE systems at US West. A number of very large telephone exchanges were also delivered to Nynex in Yonkers, north of New York City, including the world's largest AXE exchange with a capacity of more than 75,000 subscribers.

We have been gradually getting closer to and finally reached our objective of the 10% of the yearly orders, concerning new installations of local stations in the U.S.A. I suppose Ericsson is now well-known on the market. But prices have decreased at the same time as technical requirements are increasing. New services are emerging all the time and sometimes one has a feeling that everything is happening too fast.

(Dick Ryberg, former North America operations,
Ericsson Telecom, 17 February 1994)

In the beginning an organizational unit located in Sweden provided support for the US activities. In the early 1990s, however, the US organization was deemed to be competent enough and the Swedish support was divested. The Dallas organization then had all the necessary personnel, covering around 1,100 employees engaged in Public Tele-communications.

It is difficult for a foreign company to enter the U.S. market. Purchasers have a large personal responsibility and they are cautious before signing an order with a rather unknown supplier. Adaptation to the established technical standard is also arduous work, even if the established standard could imply a technological step backwards.

(Dick Ryberg, former North America operations,
Ericsson Telecom, 17 February 1994)

ERICSSON'S DIVERGENCE ON THE INTERNATIONAL MOBILE TELEPHONY MARKET

The Radio Communications business area of Ericsson operates in the field of wireless communications for civil applications and provides systems and products such as mobile telephony systems and telephones, mobile voice and data communications systems, personal paging systems and defence communications.

A complete mobile telephony (cellular radio) network consists of two main parts. One is a fixed system, with related exchanges, base radio stations and transmission equipment. The second part is comprised of mobile telephone units and related equipment. The fixed systems are normally purchased by local telephone operating companies or administrations, whereas the mobile telephone units are sold directly to subscribers.

Ericsson concentrated initially on the construction of networks in which the AXE switching system was the vital base. In 1993 Ericsson's mobile telephony systems served about 13.2 million subscribers in 64 countries (Figure 5.2), and the company continued as a world leader in this area, with a 40 per cent share of the market as regards analog systems (*Annual Report* 1993). The major part of the orders were for complements to systems that had been installed earlier.

Competitors in the systems field are Alcatel, AT&T, Motorola, NEC, Nokia, Northern Telecom and Siemens. As regards mobile telephones and equipment, there are many international and local competitors. Ericsson accounted here for a 6 per cent share of the world market in 1991.

Thus, the business area has expanded rapidly during the past decade (Tables 5.6 and 5.7). For instance, in 1984 contracts to supply systems for the construction of mobile telephony networks in sixteen countries were received. Another six countries were added in 1985.

Equipment deliveries for the Nordic Mobile Telephone network (NMT) provided an important experience:

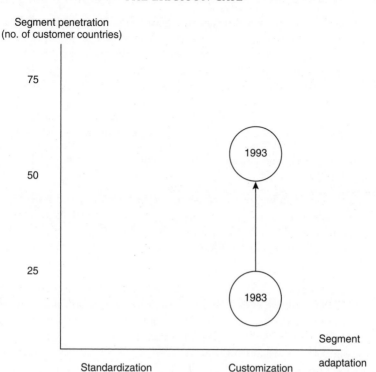

Figure 5.2 Strategic divergence of mobile telephony systems of the Radio Communications business area of Ericsson, 1983–93

Table 5.6 Summary of financial information of the Radio Communications business area of Ericsson, 1983–90 (SEK billion)

	Years							
	1983	1984	1985	1986	1987	1988	1989	1990
Net sales, external	1.6	1.9	2.5	2.7	2.8	4.7	8.1	11.6
Order bookings, external	1.9	2.3	2.6	2.4	3.3	5.1	9.3	13.3
Operating income after depreciation	31	–32	253	254	210	264	692	886

Source: Annual Reports

Besides systems, we also sell mobile telephone instruments, but the competitive factors are totally different in this sector from those in the systems sector. Production of long series and efficient distribution are decisive. Competition from around 20 manufacturers is severe. The business area has 20% of the Nordic market today.

(Åke Lundqvist, Radio Communications business area of
Ericsson, *Annual Report* 1983)

Despite tough competition, Ericsson continued expanding in the equipment sector:

We are expanding our capacity to produce terminal equipment. Competition, notably from Japanese manufacturers, is severe. But we consider our technology to be highly effective.

(Åke Lundqvist, Radio Communications business area of
Ericsson, *Annual Report* 1985)

In 1986 a new generation of mobile telephones was launched for the NMT 900 network. The new telephone, based on the so-called surface mounting technique, was a handheld mobile telephone that was no larger than a conventional telephone receiver.

Thirteen European countries agreed in 1987 to develop a common digital European system for mobile telephony, which was to be operated in the early 1990s. Ericsson, Siemens and the French company Matra signed agreements in order to develop and market this system. The following year Ericsson and Matra were chosen by a number of telecommunications network operators in Europe as the suppliers of the new Global System for Mobile communications (GSM system).

The business areas expansion caused a substantial rise in development and marketing costs. Regarding technology costs in the early 1990s, they were due to a large extent to Ericsson's simultaneous efforts to build up digital systems in Europe (GSM system), the USA (American Digital Communications system, ADC) and Japan (Japanese Digital Communications system, JDC). The USA is estimated to account for half of the world's market and is therefore a particularly important region for this business area.

Ericsson on the German mobile telephony market

In the late 1980s the German government started the deregulation of the telecommunications market. Until 1988 all telecommunication

132

Table 5.7 Summary of Ericsson's Radio Communications sales to geographic regions, 1983–93 (%)

Geographic regions	Years										
	1983	1984	1985	1986	1987	1988	1989	1990	1991	1992	1993
Europe, excl. Sweden	39	38	37	27	39	28	29	27	29	35	37
Sweden	26	26	27	18	20	26	11	7	7	8	6
USA and Canada	2	12	12	35	26	24	35	42	36	29	25
Latin America	—	—	—	—	—	—	1	3	4	6	6
Asia	31	22	20	17	6	13	12	15	19	16	19
Oceania, Australia, New Zealand	—	—	—	—	7	6	8	5	4	5	6
Africa	—	—	—	—	—	—	4	1	1	1	1

Source: Annual Reports

activities were concentrated on Deutsche Bundes Post and it was not possible for private investors to enter this market. In 1988 Deutsche Bundes Post was divided into the Post-Bank, the Postdienst and the Telekom. The Post monopoly had also been broken down and the market opened to private investors.

Due to the signing of a contract by the German government on the European GSM standard for mobile communications, a number of companies focused on the establishment of a digital network. Thus, in June 1991, Deutsche Telekom introduced in Germany the first nation-wide digital network, called the D1 network.

Another operator's licence was accessible to private investors. This concerned the nationwide digital D2 network:

> We were aware of the coming deregulation in Germany and in the autumn of 1988, we formulated a strategy for this market. To start with, we penetrated various possible operators and consortium that might perhaps get the D2-licence. This included 5–6 American alliances, 3–4 European and some German. I think that five of these were the possible future operators.
>
> We penetrated the alliances by formulating plans for marketing, technical development and network engineering that could be implemented by them. We also presented arguments that could be emphasized in the discussions with politicians. Around 80% of our resources were focused on the three most interesting.
>
> (Tomas Mikaelsson, former Ericsson Mobile
> Telekommunikation in Germany, 23 February 1994)

The licence applications that were handed in were comprehensive, before which Ericsson had presented budgetary offers to possible operators so that these should be as competitive as possible. The endeavour resulted in a licence for the Mannesmann consortium, including American interests.

The largest commercial event for the Ericsson group in 1990 (*Annual Report* 1990) was the agreement with Mannesmann Mobilfunk, covering the supply and installation of the major part of the German D2 mobile telephony network which was to be put into operation in the second half of 1991. This project extended into 1992, covering switching systems and base stations, as well as operating and support systems. In this way Ericsson had delivered its first European GSM system to Germany.

A contract with Deutsche Telekom was signed in 1991, regarding the delivery to and installation of mobile telephone equipment for the stationary network in the eastern part of Germany. In 1992 Ericsson also concluded an agreement covering volume deliveries of mobile telephones to Mannesmann. The third GSM telephone was also type-approved in Germany in December.

The race for the German E1 network for personal communications on high frequencies and using hand-portable telephones meant that Ericsson penetrated the operator, being able to send in a tender for deliveries.

> Unfortunately we did not receive an order for E1, which went to Nokia from Finland. Perhaps this was due to the links emerging between operators and suppliers. It's logical to assume that one wants several suppliers.
>
> (Tomas Mikaelsson, former Ericsson Mobile
> Telekommunikation in Germany, 23 February 1994)

Ericsson's development of the GSM technology for Europe was initiated rather early on, but no significant development resources had been established in Germany before the first order in that country. After 1991 all the necessary competence, except hardware manufacturing and parts of software design, was built up in that country. With about 300 employees, the area of mobile telephony systems dominated all Ericsson's activities in Germany.

Ericsson on the US mobile telephony market

Ericsson's activities regarding mobile telephony systems in the USA emerged from the entrepreneurial spirit of the Swedish enterprise in the early 1980s:

> When we reckoned deregulation in the U.S. was approaching, Åke Lundqvist (responsible for the Radio Systems company) sent away, among others, Leif Holm and Mats Ljunggren to probe the market and try to establish contacts with possible operators. The boys had a free hand and they were strongly supported by the management.
>
> We would help the potential operators by formulating everything, from their business plans to plans for network design and technical development. Most of these firms lacked almost everything.
>
> (Torbjörn Nilsson, Vice President, Ericsson Radio Systems,
> 23 February 1994)

In the early 1980s AT&T developed an analog standard for mobile telephony called AMPS which was similar in many respects to the Scandinavian NMT standard. This meant that, based on NMT experiences, Ericsson had the opportunity of adapting its systems to AMPS. This development work started in fact before any real orders were received and even before the American market was officially opened up.

It was known that the US market was to be divided into around 400 'Metropolitan statistical areas', covering big cities, and around 700 'rural areas'. The latter implied large geographical areas with relatively few subscribers as the potential users of mobile telephony. In each area, the relevant regional Bell company, among others, was to control one operator's licence, while a private company (a so-called Radio Common Carrier, RCC) was to control the other licence. Any Bell company was also supposed to be able to buy licences for sale in the areas outside its primary interest.

> We were aware that the adaptation of our system to AMPS had to be completed before the licences were distributed. The day after an operator received a licence he would invite tenders for systems, equipment and services, and some months later the selected system would be in operation.
>
> (Torbjörn Nilsson, Vice President, Ericsson Radio Systems,
> 23 February 1994)

Ericsson concentrated on a couple of hundred potential RCCs. One reason for this was that the Bell companies were historically tied to AT&T, Northern Telecom and Motorola. Geographically, Ericsson concentrated primarily on car-intense cities in the Northeastern and Western parts of the country. It was also considered extremely important to be able to deliver complete turnkey systems, including everything from network design to financial support.

Ericsson's expansion on the US market accelerated around 1983. In that year, strategically important orders were booked (*Annual Report* 1983). An order from the Buffalo Telephone Company for a small mobile telephony system was followed up by a contract with Rogers Radiocall, a subsidiary of the Metromedia group, to supply a system in Chicago. In 1984 local networks were ordered for Detroit and the same year Ericsson delivered one of the first RCC systems to Buffalo in the state of New York. Orders for system equipment were received in San Francisco and Houston the following year.

However, it is important to mention that the major breakthroughs were made in Chicago and Los Angeles:

Mats Ljunggren came to visit us. He said that an RCC in Los Angeles had received the second licence. If we were willing to join the competition, then we had to formulate a complete turn-key tender within a week and be prepared to put the system into operation a few months later. We discussed it during the evening and late at night, and decided that the best option was to participate, even though this involved high risks. In retrospect I think that the order that we later booked played a decisive role in our success in the U.S.

(Torbjörn Nilsson, Vice President, Ericsson Radio Systems,
23 February 1994)

McCaw Cellular Communications was one of the potential operators that Ericsson penetrated at an early stage. McCaw had the ambition to set up a nationwide mobile telephone network in the USA and extensive subscriber services. This ambition corresponded to Ericsson's own strategy and McCaw became a major customer.

One way to expand geographically was to penetrate operators in rural areas located between big cities. Thus, after the first delivery to Los Angeles valued at SEK 300 million, Ericsson also delivered a system to an operating company in San Francisco in 1986. Since then operators located between Los Angeles and San Francisco to a large extent have chosen Ericsson's systems, and the cities have been linked together. In 1987 California was almost totally covered by Ericsson's systems:

The foundations of our growth in the U.S. were laid in the middle of the 1980's. The expansion has continued since then, but the total demand exceeded the industry forecasts of the early 1980's by at least 50 times.

(Torbjörn Nilsson, Vice President, Ericsson Radio Systems,
23 February 1994)

The same pattern of expansion as in California was followed up by Texas and Florida, among other states. In the early 1990s the customer base included McCaw, Southwestern Bell, Bell South, Los Angeles Telephone Company, Pacific Telesis and Ameritech. These customers have ordered analog and digital systems. Ericsson's share of the US market was around 30 per cent, and in 1994 a couple of hundred employees were working in Dallas. These people handled primarily design, installation, service and marketing.

One of the most significant agreements in 1990 was the contract with McCaw and LIN Broadcasting Corporation, covering the expansion and upgrading of mobile telephony systems on most of their markets. Systems to be replaced included the one serving subscribers in New York and New Jersey. McCaw also replaced its systems in the Pacific Northwest with Ericsson's equipment.

The aim of the agreement with McCaw was to create a nationwide mobile telephony system in the USA (*Annual Report* 1990). Ericsson considered its competence in the related areas of switching technique, radio and network engineering as a major strength in this respect.

> We have been continually growing in a profitable way. Price competition has not been as tough, however, as in the public exchange and transmission markets. Our major competitors in the area of mobile telephony include AT&T, Motorola and Northern Telecom. But further expansion requires, in addition to satisfied customers, new concepts and the penetration of new segments.
>
> Personal Communications Services, PCS (personal communications using low battery effects and hand-portable multimedia telephones), is one of the potential areas of expansion. Most of the competitors try to position themselves in various ways. But what standards will emerge? Will it be a chaotic situation? Will consumers change their behavior?
>
> (Torbjörn Nilsson, Vice President, Ericsson Radio Systems,
> 23 February 1994)

In July 1989 a joint venture was established between Ericsson and General Electric. Some of the activities of the business area of Ericsson Radio Communications were linked together with General Electric's activities within mobile communications and in this way Ericsson GE Mobile Communications was established. Ericsson held 60 per cent and GE 40 per cent of the shares respectively (later Ericsson bought another 20 per cent). One of the advantages for Ericsson was that GE's sales and service organization was to be used. The joint venture meant that Ericsson became the second largest supplier in the world (after Motorola) of mobile communications.

The business mission of the joint venture was expressed in this way:

> To offer advanced products, systems and services for cellular mobile telephony systems in the U.S. and Canada, and for mobile company communications and mobile telephones globally.
>
> (Lars Ramqvist, Radio Communications business area of
> Ericsson, *Annual Report* 1989)

Ericsson's corporate management saw the importance of this agreement even for the business areas of Public Telecommunications and Business Communications. The major reason for this was that the basic technology in these areas is the same:

> Our cooperation with General Electric means a lot to our efforts in the U.S. Besides an access to their technology know-how and production capacity, we will acquire an understanding of how the market functions. If we had built up something on our own, it would have taken much resources in terms of time and money.
>
> (CEO Björn Svedberg, *Svenska Dagbladet* 1989)

Ericsson GE Mobile Communications opened its new development centre in Raleigh, North Carolina in the autumn of 1990. This facility was to handle development of digital mobile telephony and land mobile radio.

Ericsson on the Japanese mobile telephony market[2]

In 1985 the privatization of Nippon Telephone and Telegraph (NTT) was started and the Japanese government opened the market to foreign manufacturers. The same year Ericsson decided to open an office:

> We opened the office in Japan in order to survey the market and the technological development. Because of our lack of previous experience on that market we started by hiring people who had been living in Japan for a couple of years.
>
> (Jan Leonard, Ericsson's corporate market staff,
> 11 December 1992)

The first office was technical with three employees conducting market surveys and developing a network of business contacts. In the first years Ericsson was purchasing much more than it was selling, and this trend continued for the remaining years of the 1980s. During these first five years, sales fluctuated around SEK 25 million a year. The first products to be sold were switchboards for hotels.

When the Japanese decided to develop a system of their own for digital mobile telephone communications (the Japanese Digital Communications system, JDC), Ericsson was given an opportunity to take part in the development process. NTT invited several companies that had to draw up specifications for the system and then manufacture it in competition with each other. The American company Motorola was also involved in the development of those specifications and the manufacturing process.

In addition to NTT there are a number of private networks which have been allowed to operate. In 1992 Ericsson made deliveries to NTT and was thus firmly established with one private operator. Enthusiastically, Leonard explained:

> We are starting to get orders. In 1992 we received orders for 2 billion SEK and this is just the beginning. There are four private operators, and our market share is around 25%.
>
> (Jan Leonard, Ericsson's corporate market staff, 11 December 1992)

Operators are the companies possessing a licence allowing them to use certain frequencies in specific geographical areas. It is expected that these licences will be extended to allow for national coverage. Only four private operators covering a certain geographical area have been allowed to operate in Japan:

> It will be very difficult in the future for other competitors to enter the market, since the market is already becoming saturated, and the opportunity for entry has passed.
>
> (Jan Leonard, Ericsson's corporate market staff, 11 December 1992)

Now that Ericsson has entered the Japanese market for mobile telephone communications, it is trying to introduce other products. Leonard states:

> In 1985, when we entered the market, we did not know which products we would launch. The mobile segments were new and not well established. This made it easier to enter.
>
> (Jan Leonard, Ericsson's corporate market staff, 11 December 1992)

Before the deregulation of the Japanese market started, the market was more or less closed to foreign competitors. NTT bought only the products from their so-called NTT family, containing Japanese companies only. Later the network operators were allowed to buy from anyone they chose. Operators compete mainly by offering good services and by trying to maximize local customer satisfaction. The purchasing process usually involves comparing estimations from various companies, foreign and domestic, and choosing the one with the best quality and the lowest price. This means, of course, that competition increases, but it also allows for fairer competition between the companies involved.

During 1991–2 Ericsson extended its operations from just one office to two separate firms. The tiny technical office became a firm that started a joint venture with Toshiba in the mobile telephone area. The firm is located in Yokohama with offices in Nagoya, Tokyo and Osaka. The other corporate office is in Tokyo. In 1992 Ericsson had around eighty employees in Japan, of whom fifty to sixty were Japanese. Leonard comments that:

> Lately, since we started hiring Japanese, it has become easier to fill the gap between the cultural differences. We are still in the learning process, and the top management in Japan is still Swedish.
>
> (Jan Leonard, Ericsson's corporate market staff,
> 11 December 1992)

In the spring of 1992 Ericsson was selected by Tokyo Digital Phone to develop and instal a cellular mobile system for the Tokyo metropolitan area. The first contract was signed in May after Tokyo Digital Phone had received its operator's licence from the Ministry of Post and Telecommunications. Tokyo Digital Phone is part of a group expected to receive cellular mobile operator's licences not only for Tokyo, but also for other major areas of the country.

The system is to be built in accordance with Japanese digital cellular standards and will be installed in the Tokyo area. Ericsson was selected as the best alternative, after a careful evaluation of prospective suppliers of switch and radio equipment. Ericsson Radio Systems will be responsible for development, delivery and installation of switches and radio base stations. Development will take place in both Sweden and Japan, together with Toshiba.

The CEO of Ericsson considers Japan to be one of the most promising and important telecommunications markets in the world. At the end of 1992 there were one million mobile telephone users in Japan, which was almost as many as in Sweden at that time:

> We are hoping for lasting cooperation with Tokyo Digital Phone during the 1990's after we have made our first deliveries in 1994.
>
> (CEO Lars Ramqvist, *Affärsvärlden* 1992)

The Ericsson Toshiba joint venture will instal, maintain and service the network for the Digital Phone Group companies in Japan. This group consists of Central Japan Digital Phone, Tokyo Digital Phone and Kansai Digital Phone. In July 1992 Ericsson signed a contract with Kansai and shortly thereafter with Central Japan.

ERICSSON'S CONCENTRATION AND ADAPTATION ON THE INTERNATIONAL OFFICE AUTOMATION MARKET

This section of the chapter deals with the strategic development of Ericsson's activities on the international office automation market (an earlier version is presented in Pehrsson 1988). Until 1988, these activities were run by the Information Systems business area. The area was renamed Business Communications in 1988 and Business Networks in 1993. Ericsson Information Systems AB (EIS AB) was a subsidiary of the Ericsson group, being responsible for the Information Systems business area.

Dramatic changes in the environment and in the organization, particularly during 1984 and 1985, led to the choice of the concentration strategy. The Communications systems that came into focus covered products such as subscriber exchanges and data networks for offices.

The financial information concerning this business area is shown in Table 5.8. Table 5.9 illustrates the distribution of shares of the invoicing by geographic region. In Table 5.10 figures concerning sales of business elements in the Information Systems business area are presented.

In 1985 Stig Larsson who had been working for Ericsson for a long period of time became responsible for the company Ericsson Information Systems and was made head of the corresponding business area. He initiated careful investigations regarding the capability of the organization, which showed that a revised business strategy was necessary. In accordance with the new concentration strategy, Stig Larsson started an action programme in order to implement it and to improve the financial results. The business area's invoicing was around SEK 9 billion in 1986 with almost 17,000 people employed.

Table 5.8 Summary of financial information of the Business Communications business area (1988–90) and the Information Systems business area of Ericsson (1983–7) (SEK billion)

| | Years | | | | | | | |
	1983	1984	1985	1986	1987	1988	1989	1990
Net sales, external	7.5	9.0	10.0	9.2	9.2	3.5	4.9	4.8
Order bookings, external	8.0	9.8	9.9	8.9	9.0	4.1	4.9	4.7
Operating income after depreciation	237	−217	−806	−284	−58	155	252	148

Source: Annual Reports

Table 5.9 Summary of Ericsson's Business Networks sales to geographic regions (1993), sales of Business Communications (1988–92) and sales of the Information Systems business area (1983–7) (%)

Geographic regions	Years										
	1983	1984	1985	1986	1987	1988	1989	1990	1991	1992	1993
Europe, excl. Sweden	45	51	52	60	60	60	60	67	69	75	70
Sweden	28	26	25	24	25	8	10	5	4	3	3
USA and Canada	13[1]	9	7	6	5	8	7	4	4	3	2
Latin America	6	6	7	4	4	10	8	9	8	7	6
Asia	6	4	3	3	3	4	5	6	6	7	14
Oceania, Australia, New Zealand	—	3	5	3	3	8	10	8	8	5	4
Africa	2	1	1	—	—	—	—	1	1	—	1

Source: Annual Reports
Note:
1 Including Oceania

Table 5.10 Summary of sales of Ericsson's Information Systems business area to external customers by business element, 1983–7 (%)

Business elements	Years		Business elements	Years		
	1983	*1984*		*1985*	*1986*	*1987*
Office equipment	24	13	Communications systems[1]	34	35	35
Communication systems	21	21	Computer systems[2]	39	42	45
Work stations	19	30	Office equipment[3]	25	21	20
Business systems	17	15	Miscellaneous	2	2	—
Computer peripherals	7	9				
Security and telesystems	6	7				
Miscellaneous	6	5				

Source: Annual Reports
Notes:
1 Large MD 110 subscriber exchanges, Eripax data networks, modems, small subscriber exchanges, intercom systems, telephone instruments.
2 Data terminals, personal computers, small business systems/minicomputers, bank terminal systems.
3 Printers, typewriters, calculators, office furniture.

In 1984 the Information Systems business area contained a wide range of products, from standardized products like office furniture to advanced computerized systems. The penetrated segments contained everything from individual consumers to large companies and authorities.

At the end of 1987 the range of products had been narrowed down to those that had to do with telecommunications systems and advanced computerized systems. This meant that the customer target group now consisted of relatively large organizations which were inclined to give priority to suppliers with the capacity to deliver complete systems. Concentration was also conducted to Western Europe.

Thus, the broadening of the Ericsson group's product and market scope in the early 1980s did not produce the intended financial results. The Information Systems business area was created during that period, by adding the acquired companies to the two existing divisions (the information systems and the subscriber equipment divisions) of the Public Telecommunications business area. Broadly speaking, this was done in order to penetrate the office automation market.

When Stig Larsson entered the scene as the business area manager, the new concentration strategy implied focusing on traditional knowledge based on the development and marketing of advanced communications systems for large organizations. At the beginning of 1988 most of the product groups that did not belong to the core of the group's activities had been divested. Thus, Ericsson concentrated and adapted its activities on the international office automation market (Figure 5.3). After the description of the process underlying this development, the final part of this section will deal in more detail with the business strategy of the Business Communications area, with the focus on the activities on the German market.

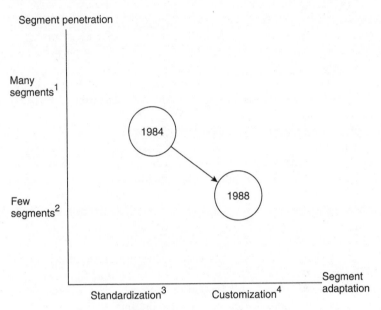

Figure 5.3 Strategic concentration and adaptation of the business area of Ericsson Information Systems, 1984–8

Notes:
1 Individual consumers and all organization types
2 Large organizations
3 Customized communication systems, 21 per cent
4 Customized communications, 100 per cent

Business strategy of Ericsson Information Systems from 1982

At the end of the 1970s the Ericsson group had managed the transition from electromechanical technology to electronic technology in the area of telecommunication products and systems. Extensive knowledge

145

regarding computer technology had been built up. The AXE telephone exchange system was generating profit, which is why the corporate management considered the financial strength to be sufficient to start decreasing dependence on customers such as national public telecommunication administrations. Estimations in the industry showed a relatively slow growth rate of 5 per cent per year in this market during the 1980s. As the accessible part of the public market seemed also to be decreasing due to protectionistic tendencies all over the world, Ericsson started looking for new markets.

The management gave a lot of thought to the situation concerning information technology (telecommunication, office equipment and computer technology). The private market for office automation seemed to promise certain opportunities. The corporate management of Ericsson saw that this market segment was technically related to the area of telecommunication and, therefore, the already existing know-how could form the basis for new development. Marketing competence needed to be extended, however, and the product range widened in order to attract the private market for office automation.

This is why the Swedish company Datasaab was acquired. Datasaab and two of the former divisions of the group's parent company LM Ericsson formed the foundations of the new company Ericsson Information Systems AB, which was formally established on 1 January 1982. The turnover of the company was around SEK 3 billion in 1982 and the number of employees totalled 4,000. Håkan Ledin was appointed as the company's President.

The LM Ericsson divisions for subscriber equipment and information systems were established at the end of the 1970s, offering products such as telephone exchanges to private customers. The products were based on telecommunication technology and they were supplemented by Datasaab's workplace terminals and small computers in an effort to create a range of products that would be attractive to EIS AB.

After widening the range of products, the business mission of the Ericsson group was formulated in this manner:

> To fulfil the market's need for products, systems and services within the areas of telecommunications and information systems.
>
> (Ericsson's group staff of strategic planning, internal paper,
> November 1983)

The foundation of Ericsson Information Systems was regarded as a 'logical step' in the strategic development of the group (CEO Björn Svedberg, *Annual Report* 1982). One of the goals was to increase the share of the group invoicing concerning private customers from around 20 per cent in 1981 to 40 per cent in 1985. The business area Information Systems, which was controlled by EIS AB and also consisted of a number of other companies, was to become as large as the major business area of Public Telecommunications at the end of the referred five-year period.

The general estimations in the industry in 1981 regarding the total industry volume of information technology on the private market showed a yearly increase of 15 per cent during the remaining part of the 1980s. This was three times as large an increase as the expected growth rate for the public market. When it comes to individual products on the private market, the following annual growth rates (per cent) during 1981–5 were forecast by Ericsson's management (internal market analysis, EIS AB 1981).

- equipment for wordprocessing   32
- workplace terminals   28
- consulting services   20
- other terminals   13
- small computers   12
- networks and other telecommunication equipment 9
- large computers   4

The value of the total world market for information technology was estimated to be around SEK 50 billion in 1980. Large computers, telecommunication equipment and consulting services dominated in terms of market value. As regards the geographical distribution of the world market, 50 per cent was located in the USA, with Western Europe and Japan accounting for approximately 30 per cent and 10 per cent respectively. The situation was summarized in an internal report:

> Office work has to be more effective. In an effort to increase productivity, telecommunications technology has to be integrated with computer technology. Telephones, exchange equipment and other relevant technology will be integrated with word processing equipment into information systems that rely on networks. The market for totally integrated systems will develop slowly during the 1980's, however, considering the fact that customer needs are still inadequately defined, that there is always inertia and resistance to change, and that legal restrictions on telecommunications exist.
>
> (Internal market analysis, EIS AB 1981)

Ericsson Information Systems intended to keep its rate of volume growth at the same level as that of the total world market, which meant an annual growth rate of 15 per cent during the 1980s. The volume growth for specific products was supposed to follow the expected annual world growth rate. In each combination of product, customer segment and country the aim was to reach a high market share of more than 20 per cent. The company was expected to start generating profits from 1984 onwards. In the first phase of the new business area, the growth objective was put forward at the expense of the profit objective. The intention was to put more stress on profits at a later date.

In order to exploit the office automation market Ericsson strived for an integration of telecommunications, computer technology and office equipment, so that complete systems for information handling at individual workplaces could be offered. In this context, information means data, text, voice and image. Information handling comprises storage, processing, transmission and presentation.

Integrated information systems were to be linked together by networks that stem from a telephone exchange similar to the MD 110. Here, the same basic AXE technology as the one offered to public customers was to be applied. In fact, the MD 110 system was regarded as the major competitive advantage on entry to the office automation market. Various subsystems like, for example, conventional analog and digital telephones can be connected to MD 110. This is a digital exchange system designed for a large number of connections. As MD 110 is suitable for both analog and digital environments, integration of voice and datacommunication is facilitated. MD 110 is being continuously developed and refined and in 1983 this was costing around SEK 200 million.

The aim of Ericsson Information Systems was gradually to become an integrated systems supplier. During the first years, marketing was to be concerned with separate products. The move towards integrated systems around individual workplaces was to be managed by replacing products and complementing the product programmes as the customers' needs gradually emerged and matured.

However, major differences between marketing to public and private customers were noticed. In an internal market analysis (EIS AB 1981) the characteristics of marketing to public customers were summarized:

- about one hundred customers in the world;
- very large orders;
- very competent buyers;

- long-term relations between selling companies and buyers;
- the same basic technology for telephone systems is applied for decades.

When it comes to the private sector, the following features emerged:

- several hundred thousand customers;
- variation of order sizes;
- skilled or ignorant buyers;
- short-term relations between selling companies and buyers;
- short product life cycles, of perhaps only five years.

The growing market for information technology attracted various types of competitors, a good many of whom were very large. In 1979, Ericsson held the twenty-second position on the world's turnover ranking list. Of the world's top fifty companies dealing in information technology twenty-five were US owned (Honeywell, IBM, ITT, Western Electric, Xerox, etc.); nine were Japanese owned (Fujitsu, Hitachi, NEC, Toshiba, etc.); six were UK owned (GEC, ICL, Thorn-EMI, etc.).

Considering that Ericsson Information Systems was competing on the private market, management came to two major conclusions. In the first place, a large sales force had to be hired and trained for a competitive environment. Second, new products and systems had to be developed at a faster rate. This demanded that production had to be able to adjust quickly to new demands.

At the end of 1982 the Swedish company Facit was acquired by Ericsson. This company had been manufacturing and marketing office equipment such as calculators and office furniture, primarily for mass consumption. One reason for the acquisition of Facit was that Ericsson wished quickly to build up distribution channels in order to reach private customers. As Facit possessed fairly well-functioning channels, the management perceived synergy possibilities.

The acquisition of Facit implied that the number of customer types had increased, now ranging from large companies and public authorities to individual consumers. Furthermore, since it was desirable closely to integrate the two former LM Ericsson divisions, Datasaab and Facit, three organizational cultures now had to be considered. Before the acquisition of Facit, the business area of Ericsson Information Systems was organized as illustrated in Figure 5.4.

The Communication Systems division was responsible for the MD 110 telephone switching system, various switching devices and networks. Dataprocessing systems for business and banking applications

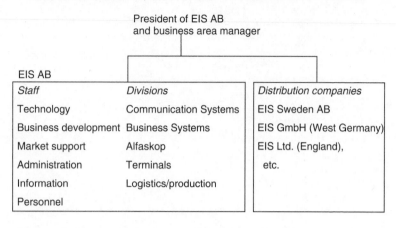

Figure 5.4 Organizational structure of the Information Systems business area of Ericsson, 1982

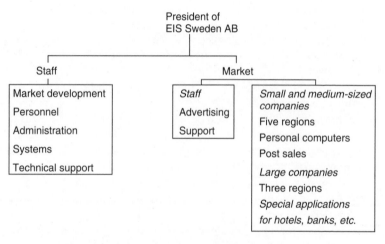

Figure 5.5 Organizational structure of the distribution company EIS Sweden AB, 1982

constituted the main product types of the Business Systems division, while the Alfaskop division dealt mostly with terminals for mainframe communication as well as communication with other computer types. The Terminal division was concerned primarily with telephone apparatus and support systems (e.g. wordprocessing for offices).

As Figure 5.4 indicates, production was separated from the product divisions. The main reason for this was the similarity of the products' components, which usually facilitates large-scale production.

The staffs concerned with technology, business development, market support and administration were involved in various degrees in the planning of activities for divisions and distribution units.

The distribution companies acted as tentacles on the market, one of whose organizational structure, EIS Sweden AB, is described in Figure 5.5. As these companies were generally responsible for profit, they would have a major influence on their own structure. However, the structure had to comply as much as possible with the market strategy laid out by EIS AB.

Distribution companies represented in many cases more than one business area of the Ericsson group, although one area was responsible as regards profitability for the distribution company in question.

In 1983 the initial business strategy of the Information Systems business area had become more explicit and was presented in the following way by the manager responsible, Håkan Ledin:

> Demands for efficient information handling are increasing. As a result, a new industry is emerging, based on the integration of data processing, office automation and telecommunications. The area of telecommunication is viewed as the critical element: today's communications networks must not only handle telecommunications in the traditional sense of the term – the transmission of voice, data and images – but must also provide access to the computers in the network.
>
> A number of companies are trying in various ways to establish their position in the field of information technology. We have here the traditional, large computer manufacturers who are seeking to acquire communications know-how through their own development work as well as by cooperation agreements; and we have certain telecommunications companies, including Ericsson, who – based on their telecommunication know-how – are making products and masters in the field of information handling.
>
> Ericsson's business concept focuses on the combination of distributed data processing, work terminals and telecommunications. The personal computer made its breakthrough in 1983, which underscores the importance of focusing on work stations and confirms the trend towards less dependence on large central computers.

The Information Systems business area's sales amounted to 7.2 billion SEK in 1983, the dominant market being Europe. Its profitability targets have not been reached yet, although the operating results have been improving faster than it was forecasted when the investments were begun.

Ericsson Information Systems AB, the largest unit in the business area, is now divided into four sectors: Communications Systems, Business Systems, Terminal Equipment and Office Equipment. The area includes also companies engaged in the development and marketing of specialty products.

Communications Systems include the MD 110 digital sub-scriber exchange (PABX), the ERIPAX data transmission system and ERIMAIL, a system for storing and transmitting text. They constitute the basis of systematized information handling and are supplemented by terminals and computer systems. Intensive development work is under way and this sector is expected to continue growing in volume at an annual rate of at least 20 per cent for the next few years.

In the U.S., Ericsson is gaining technical and marketing experience from the integration of communications and terminal equipment. A supply agreement with the U.S. company Honey-well Inc. has been entered into, covering the resale of the business area's communications systems through Honeywell's marketing organization. A joint-venture development company has been also formed for the adaptation of these systems to the American requirements and for their further development. This company employs 150 qualified engineers.

Because Ericsson possesses the necessary know-how in the areas of telecommunications and data processing, we have a very good platform for growth – when compared with many other competitors – especially as regards the gradual integration of various phases of the informations systems. Very few of our competitors can boast of such combined know-how within their own organizations. They are therefore forced to seek cooperation with other companies to achieve the necessary coordination of activities.

Our business concept, which is directed towards being able to sell complete integrated systems towards the end of the 1980's, requires a stable customer base. We are therefore continuing the rapid development of Ericsson's sales organization in Europe. The sales companies in the Nordic countries are developing fast, in terms of both growth and earnings. We are continuing our efforts in strengthening our position in Great Britain, France and Italy. The expansion in West Germany has been particularly rapid.

New business opportunities are being created as a result of the change that is taking place in the telecommunications market in the U.S. There, in contrast to our market strategy in Europe, we are concentrating on the sales of few products, with emphasis on the communications area.

The Business Systems, Terminal Equipment and Office Equipment sectors were the primary contributors to the favourable development of the business area, while the Communications sector continues to incur very heavy development costs. These expenditures will pay off by higher sales of the newly introduced systems in 1984.

(Håkan Ledin, Annual Report 1983)

The situation changes

During the first two years (i.e. 1982 and 1983) the business area of Information Systems showed positive financial results. As Table 4.8 shows, the profit in 1983 amounted to SEK 237 million. The following year did not show any profit. As the total size of orders increased by 26 per cent and the total invoicing grew by only 15 per cent (*Annual Report* 1984), internal problems obviously must have appeared when trying to deliver the orders. Regarding the invoicing, the management estimated a 24 per cent increase in 1984.

Poor financial results were shown in the half-year report in 1984 presented by the Ericsson group. The profit forecast had to be adjusted downwards, which was understood to have been caused partly by the heavy development costs for the Information Systems business area.

External observers attributed the problems to Ericsson's prioritization of volume growth at the expense of short-term profitability. The sales personnel had obviously accepted too many commitments, which could not be carried out by the remaining personnel. This led to delivery delays and a situation in which large amounts of capital were tied up in various inventories.

The problems concerned primarily the area's main products (i.e. the subscriber exchange MD 110, banking terminals and personal computers). For these products, invoicing lagged behind because of the difficulties in coordination of product development activities and scarcity of components. In fact, a shortage of electronic components characterized the entire information technology industry.

Ericsson Information Systems AB, the most prominent company in this business area, did not behave as a homogeneous company after the merger between the two divisions of LM Ericsson, Datasaab and Facit. To a large extent, common working routines were still lacking. One example shows that the same product was given different order numbers, which caused confusion in deliveries. The absence of a stable organization became evident when four new products were simultaneously introduced on the market: MD 110, a new banking terminal system, a new mini computer and a new personal computer. The CEO reacted soon enough:

> We need more discipline in EIS, where one has gone in for too many things at the same time. Now the short-term profitability has to be taken into consideration as well.
>
> (CEO Björn Svedberg, *Veckans Affärer* 1984)

As time went on, other members of the organization gradually became aware of the seriousness of the situation. The CEO stated again:

> As we see it now, the EIS puzzle was totally a question of mismanagement. Earlier, I sometimes regarded myself as being too conservative when I did not agree with new projects of EIS. Now I am sorry that I did not put an end to a number of those projects earlier on.
>
> (CEO Björn Svedberg, *Veckans Affärer* 1985b)

> When we were buying Datasaab and Facit we believed in a quick integration of the systems, following the idea of 'The Office of the Future', where everything was meant to be linked together. However, the reality does not evolve as quickly as one thought.
>
> (CEO Björn Svedberg, *Dagens Industri* 1985)

The Chairman of the Board of the parent company LM Ericsson gave his view:

> I was not really so surprised by the EIS problems. This could be expected since the expansion was so rapid. One part of the problem was that monthly financial reports were missing. Another part was the way in which the changed situation was presented externally. A more effective, early warning system could have facilitated the explanation to foreign investors, and at the same time one could emphasize the importance of the investment in Ericsson's future.
>
> (Chairman of the Board Hans Werthen, *Veckans Affärer* 1985b)

A more official problem description was given in the *Annual Report* (1984):

> The fast volume expansion of the business areas of Information Systems and Radio Communications mainly made the planning of production difficult and caused a high increase in costs during the second half of 1984. A defective cost control, particularly in Information Systems as well as difficulties in integrating three accounting systems after the merger made the problems worse.
>
> The causes of the problems on the whole were something that the business areas' management were able to control. The causes were related to the fast expansion and a certain underestimation of the accompanying difficulties.
>
> Investment in informations systems is, however, necessary. Companies that put themselves outside the integration of communications systems and office equipment will become less competitive.
>
> The Ericsson group has undergone major changes during the 1980s. Our working premises today differ quite dramatically from those of yesterday. The product life cycles are shorter, the growth rate is higher, the competition is harder and the risks are higher. But the opportunities are considerably larger.
>
> (CEO Björn Svedberg, *Annual Report* 1984)

As from 1 October 1984, there was a shift of managers within the business areas of the Ericsson group. Håkan Ledin, the previous Information Systems manager, was replaced, being appointed instead as manager of Ericsson, Inc. in the USA.

Stig Larsson who was earlier in charge of the Group's component company now became President of Ericsson Information Systems AB, being also responsible for the business area. Stig Larsson initiated a revision of the business strategy and a comprehensive action programme in order to increase profitability:

> The first thing I did was to project the nine months' result for EIS on the whole year and compare it with the budget for 1985. Between the projection and the budget there was a large gap, and step by step we are now implementing actions in order to close the gap.
>
> When the construction problems have been solved, we have good products that are in demand on the market. But we have to create a profitable organization that surrounds the products.

155

As regards marketing activities we concentrate harder on the industrial world and in particular on Western Europe. We speak more calmly about the objectives on the U.S. market.

(Stig Larsson, *Veckans Affärer* 1985a)

The action programme consisted of the following major activities:

1 *Review of the organization.* All the units of the matrix organization went through all its organizational features such as working routines, distribution of responsibility, product range and market organization.

2 *Reorganization.* In order to create more distinct areas of responsibility and a more effective resource utilization, three divisions were established within the EIS company: Communication Systems, Computer Systems and Office Equipment. These divisions became responsible for product development, as well as production and marketing. They were to be coordinated by a group of directors, including the President and ten other senior managers.

3 *General cost reduction.* It was decided that employment of new personnel was to be prohibited, except for constructors. Sales of office equipment were stopped in eleven regional markets and sales of typewriters were ceased in fifty regional markets. The so-called non-strategic activities like, for example, manufacturing of office furniture were divested.

4 *Product development and production were made more effective.* The know-how from other parts of the Ericsson group was to be transferred to Information Systems. Skilled technicians from Public Telecommunications were engaged to solve problems.

5 *Market concentration.* Sales were concentrated to large and middle-sized customers, especially in Western Europe.

6 *Monthly balancing of the books.* As from 1 January 1985, all units responsible for profits were to present monthly balancing of the books.

7 *Individual talks with the personnel.* In the so-called planning talks the management discussed with a large number of employees what they should really concentrate on.

The revised business strategy as from 1986

In 1986 the focal point of the Information Systems business area became the general knowledge amalgamated by the Ericsson group regarding construction of systems within the area of telecommunication and advanced electronic systems. The main argument here was that customers were interested in the first place in manufacturers which possessed the knowledge and the capacity to deliver complete systems (*Annual Report* 1985). Thus, technical concentration was performed in order to meet a forthcoming integration of speech and data functions. With regard to marketing, the aim was set to become a leading supplier of subscriber exchanges and workplace equipment for offices of large and middle-sized customers, primarily in Western Europe. As regards markets outside Europe, especially the USA, sales were to be concentrated on products such as the MD 110 subscriber exchange and were to be carried out by wholly owned subsidiaries.

The three divisions of the EIS company: Communication Systems (34 per cent of the external invoicing in 1985), Computer Systems (39 per cent) and Office Equipment (25 per cent), corresponded in principle to the earlier divisions of LM Ericsson, Datasaab and Facit respectively. The new divisions were responsible for the following major products:

- Communication Systems. Large subscriber exchanges (MD 110), small subscriber exchanges, Eripax data network, modems, telephone apparatus.
- Computer Systems. Workplace terminals, personal computers, mini computers, banking systems.
- Office Equipment. Writers, typewriters, calculators.

The business area manager Stig Larsson presented his view of the causes of the weak financial performance of the Information Systems business area in 1985. The losses (SEK 806 million) also included restructuring costs:

> The causes of the business area's problems are rooted in a very fast growth in the 1980's, as well as in product development under severe time restrictions and an unexpectedly fast decrease in demand in 1985. Control systems for product development and logistics were insufficient and were not able to meet these changes.
>
> Our work with the restructuring also included an overhaul of administrative routines. We have improved our forecasts, a new and more effective accounting system is being developed and the logistic routines are improving. A conservative cost control and a number of cost reduction measures mean that the number of employees of the business area will be reduced by 2,000 persons. In 1985 the number was reduced by about 1,000 persons, starting from the level of 22,000.

The restructuring plan also means an increased stress on the core of our business mission: to offer products, systems and services for transmission and handling of speech, data, image and text, mainly to large and middle-sized customers in Europe.

(Stig Larsson, *Annual Report* 1985)

In order to improve the financial performance the number of employees in the remaining parts of the business area was reduced by about 4,000 during 1986. In addition, the use of capital in production and inventories was made highly effective. Other efforts to increase the turnover rate of capital consisted of a substantial reduction of accounts receivable and interest expenses. All these efforts resulted in an improved financial performance, so that in 1986 the losses were reduced to SEK 284 million. For 1987 and 1988 the management were expecting profits.

The CEO reflects upon the rather dramatic development of the EIS company and its business area:

The losses and the negative cash flow of the EIS were a serious matter, but the group as a whole was never in danger. There are many resources that we have never utilized. The patient was seriously ill, but now it is undergoing a recovery.

(CEO Björn Svedberg, *Veckans Affärer* 1987)

The concentration continued and in the autumn of 1987 a part corresponding to approximately 20 per cent of the business area's turnover, equivalent to SEK 2 billion, was sold. This included the production of typewriters based on text processing, calculators and writers and the Facit company. The production of office furniture was also sold.

What we are selling is located on the border of our concerns. We are divesting activities which do not fit in with the things we should be really concentrating on.

(Stig Larsson, *Svenska Dagbladet* 1987)

The return to the Ericsson group's traditional competence regarding development and manufacture of advanced technical systems took place in January 1988. At that time it became known that the Finnish company Nokia had bought the Computer Systems division. As a compensation, Ericsson became a partner of Nokia, controlling 20 per cent of its shares. Björn Svedberg pictured the following background:

At the end of the 1970's our AXE-system was successful on the market. As we wanted to accomplish more than this, and it was important to be able to deliver complete office systems, we established Ericsson Information Systems. However, various problems related to the products emerged soon enough.

This was the beginning of a tough period, but we worked hard and got results. We realize now that we do not have to manufacture data terminals in order to deliver complete systems. Standardization has made it possible to incorporate other terminals into our systems. When we later realized that expansion was necessary, we made an offer to Nokia as regards the Computer Systems division.

(CEO Björn Svedberg, *Svenska Dagbladet* 1988)

The remaining part of the Information Systems business area was to concentrate mainly on subscriber exchanges, data networks and telephone apparatus. In January 1988 about 7,000 people were employed in this business area. To mark a new beginning, the area was renamed Ericsson Business Communications.

Ericsson on the German office automation market

The revised business strategy of Ericsson Information Systems implied focusing on communications systems and concentrating on large and middle-sized customers in Western Europe. From this point of view the German market is interesting, considering its large number of potential customers.

Earlier on, due to the current legal restrictions on telecommunications and the relative closeness of the former West German market, Ericsson had not actively tried to penetrate that market. The group only set up its first outlet in West Germany at the beginning of the 1980s, when Ericsson Information Systems opened a sales office in Düsseldorf. This became the start for the setting up of a sales organization:

Our business mission is to be able to offer totally integrated information systems at the end of the 1980's, which requires a stable customer basis. Therefore, we continue the fast expansion of our sales organization in Europe. . . . The growth has been particularly fast in West Germany.

(Håkan Ledin, responsible for the business area of Ericsson Information Systems, *Annual Report* 1983)

Even though the organizational expansion had been achieved, it took time to get properly established on the German market. At the beginning

159

of 1986, Europe as a whole accounted for 78 per cent of the business area's invoicing, but West Germany's share was still rather small. Later that year a few large orders were received and Stig Larsson, the new business area manager, declared that a breakthrough on the important West German market had been achieved (*Annual Report* 1986).

By June 1987, one million MD 110 extensions had been delivered to all the markets since the system was first presented. There was a celebration when a West German company ordered the system. Ericsson regarded it as a symbol of growing success on what was referred to as 'the very tough West German market' (*Annual Report* 1987). Further, Lufthansa and the University of Bremen became two other important customers that bought MD 110 in 1988.

As a point of comparison, a total of 900,000 MD 110 extensions were installed in 1990 and 800,000 in 1989 (*Annual Report* 1990). Additionally, in 1990 300,000 extensions of smaller subscriber exchanges were installed by Ericsson. The total of world installations in 1990 covered 13 million extensions, which gave Ericsson an 8.5 per cent market share. Ericsson Business Communications accounted for a base of the total of 4 million MD 110 extensions installed in 1990.

As major parts of the activities of the Information Systems business area were divested in 1988 and the remaining activities were renamed Ericsson Business Communications, the West German company was named Ericsson Business Communications GmbH. Heinrich Thanscheidt was appointed President of this sales company which employed fifty people. (In 1991 150 persons were employed, including 20 salesmen.) In general, the products are bought in from Sweden, while the sales company is responsible for marketing and service on the local market.

The subscriber exchange MD 110 and the ERIPAX data network make up the main products. The customer base includes ABB in Mannheim, Axel Springer Verlag, the Stock Exchange in Frankfurt, Deutsche Sparkasse, the University of Bremen and the University of Erlangen.

The problems that had led to the divestment of Ericsson Information Systems became known on the West German market and caused a somewhat confused image:

> The problems experienced by Ericsson Information Systems became well-known, even in West Germany. The newspapers scrutinized us and we got a bad reputation. Since then we have been consciously working on building up positive customer

relations. We want to create an image that reflects professionalism, reliability and service-mindness. Our subsidiary in that country has been run since 1988 by a local manager who knows the industry.

(Gunnar Wiklund, manager International Operations, Ericsson Business Communications, February 1991)

For Gunnar Wiklund the target group was made up of small and medium-sized companies, as well as banks and universities. Heinrich Thanscheidt, in charge of the German subsidiary, gave prominence to two other target groups: large, geographically spread organizations such as universities, and organizations which could be reached through previously established cable networks. In such networks, operation companies rent space and engage equipment suppliers such as Ericsson Business Communications. When it comes to universities, geographical expansion is a common feature, creating a need for subscriber exchanges and data networks. Universities are also important references for potential customers.

It is difficult to further segment the market. Organizations that need subscriber exchanges with more than 150 extensions make up a large enough segment.

(Heinrich Thanscheidt, Ericsson Business Communications in Germany, May 1991)

In the early 1990s the annual German demand for subscriber exchanges corresponded to roughly 500,000 extensions.

One hundred thousand MD 110 extensions a year can be considered a solid base, and this is our objective. It is the same as a 20% market share.

(Heinrich Thanscheidt, Ericsson Business Communications in Germany, May 1991)

Customers are penetrated primarily without any intermediaries. In this way, a national network of branch offices is being built up. In May 1991 new offices were established in Berlin, Frankfurt, Hannover, München and Stuttgart. Earlier on, cooperation had been established with small and large retail dealers controlling the stores. These retailers were then responsible for customer relations, while Ericsson stood for the execution of orders.

As we primarily offer large systems we penetrate the whole of Germany. We are also interested in the former East Germany and

161

since August 1990, we are represented by a branch office in Berlin.

(Heinrich Thanscheidt, Ericsson Business Communications in Germany, May 1991)

Twenty-nine companies covering eighty-four large subscriber exchanges have received permission to use certain frequencies by the official authority that controls this area in Germany. Thus, the competition is intense and prices are pushed down:

As long as new competitors come into the industry, there will be price competition. For example, when Philips and Nixdorf entered the scene in 1985 prices fell and since then they have stayed at the same level. At present, Northern Telecom from Canada has low prices in Germany. And what about NEC, the Japanese company, that manufactures small subscriber exchanges in Germany? Will they go for large exchanges as well? And AT&T from the U.S.A.?

(Heinrich Thanscheidt, Ericsson Business Communications in Germany, May 1991)

To survive the competition, many industry competitors choose to cooperate and even to merge fully. The cooperation between the two German companies Siemens and Nixdorf is one example:

I regard the marriage between Siemens and Nixdorf as being good for us. There is one competitor less to meet. Furthermore, Nixdorf's old customers will be nervous when they realize that their need for services is not a major priority any more.

(Heinrich Thanscheidt, Ericsson Business Communications in Germany, May 1991)

The supply of services is one of the main competitive means. The market leader Siemens has at its disposal large service resources. By dealing with Siemens its customers have become used to extensive services, which in turn put pressure on small competitors like Ericsson Business Communications. Despite this, Ericsson tries to emphasize technical features of its products in the first place:

We put forward the technical features of our products. It is difficult for us to sell packages of products. It is not easy either to establish long-term customer relations. Germany is not Ericsson's home market and we do not have old established relations on this market. In fact, our largest problem here is to

162

build up something that can be called a stable home market. Like Siemens, Telenorma and nowadays also Bundes Post Telekom.
(Heinrich Thanscheidt, Ericsson Business Communications
in Germany, May 1991)

Ericsson Business Communications GmbH was consolidated in 1993–4 and became a part of Ericsson Deutschland GmbH, responsible for a 'division' for private customers.

NOTES

1 The methodology of the in-depth study was designed, in principle, as follows. The starting-point consisted of the studies on Ericsson that I had conducted earlier (Pehrsson 1985, 1988, 1991, 1993). Secondary data from business journals, newspapers and annual reports were then compiled in chronological order following the basic framework of this book. Furthermore, I carried out seven personal interviews with executives who had been personally involved in strategy development in Germany, the USA and Japan respectively.

Two interviews were done within the Public Telecommunications business area, three concerned Radio Communications (one of which was carried out by two MBA students from Stockholm University), and the remaining two dealt with Business Communications. The interviews followed a structured procedure, in which the reference points were provided by the framework of the book. The interviews were typed out, giving the respondents an opportunity to comment on the information.

2 This section was initially prepared in January 1993 by Per Inglander and Veronica Stewart, MBA students at Stockholm University.

6

A DISCUSSION OF ERICSSON'S DEVELOPMENT OF INTERNATIONAL BUSINESS STRATEGIES

Following the framework given by the strategic states model and the theoretical reviews provided in the first part of the book, this chapter presents a discussion of Ericsson's strategy development. First, three important choices will be highlighted – choices concerning the focus on telecommunications systems and the accompanying customization, and the choice of a penetration of a variety of market segments. Second, more concrete manifestations of strategy development will be exemplified. The establishment of customer relations and the formation of strategic alliances that facilitate market entry constitute in this context a manifestation of customer divergence and geographic divergence.

ERICSSON'S CHOICES IN RELATION TO THE STRATEGIC STATES MODEL

Once an offer has been identified as consisting primarily of separate products, or of systems of products, the strategic states model stipulates two central choices of strategy: number of market segments that are to be penetrated and the degree of segment adaptation. Ericsson has chosen to focus on telecommunications systems, which are by nature highly adaptable to the needs of customers in single segments. As regards the systems for public networks and mobile telephony, the customer divergence strategy is clearly present. This means that Ericsson intends to establish relationships with network operators of different types (i.e. with customers located in different segments of the market).

Focus on telecommunications systems and customization

An important ingredient of LM Ericsson's strategy was, right from its very beginnings, to develop products and concepts related to telephone technology. Thinking in terms of systems has gradually evolved, and efforts to concentrate on systems have been intensified during the last decades. In the 1990s, systems for public telecommunications, mobile telephony and business communications constituted the primary focus. The major systems include the AXE switching system for public telecommunications, the mobile telephony systems and the MD 110 subscriber exchange for offices. In mobile telephony, AXE constitutes the system's exchange. Ericsson also offers radio base stations and telephones.

Due to the rise in development costs of hardware and software there is a need for as great a standardization of products as possible. In principle, Ericsson designs systems that allow the replacement of single components. Customized components are produced mainly by Ericsson, and standardized components by subcontractors.

The prerequisite for continuous development of the AXE system was established by the initial selection of a modular and flexible system structure, adaptable to changing requirements. The objective was to introduce new functions and increase the potential range of services in networks already installed. Furthermore, the MD 110 was built around linked modules, where each module can function as an independent exchange. AXE's function, software modularity and other technical features are located in the MD 110 exchange for office use.

Thus, Ericsson's knowledge of telecommunications systems can be regarded as a core competence, which has made possible strategic development characterized by entry into technically related areas. The same type of strategy was obviously intended for the international office automation market. Based on its technological know-how, Ericsson formed here a broad product range, covering both simple and complex products, as well as systems for office automation. The heterogeneous customer types encountered on this market differed very much from what Ericsson had been familiar with. This is a main explanation of the strategy process which finally resulted in a concentration on more familiar customer types and adaptation to their requirements.

The building of long-term customer relations is an important aspect of systems marketing. One manifestation of this is the fact that the major part of Ericsson's orders concern prolonged orders complementing the existing systems, managed by network operators.

One of Ericsson's wishes is to establish long-term relations with both traditional and new operators of different types, especially with large operators demanding relatively large volumes. A customization strategy is clearly discernible here, since one is trying to determine the requirements of each operator type and adjust the capability to develop technical and financial solutions.

However, the extent to which customization and standardization should be applied is generally a problematic choice (Pehrsson 1993). If customization goes too far, scale effects will be difficult to obtain. On the other hand, pure standardization implies vulnerability to price competition. The balance between the customization of a system and its standardization in an effort to reach reproducibility is, in fact, the major problem of 'systems' companies. Ericsson's way of dealing with this problem is to adhere to the modularity principle of its systems. Customized and standardized components form modules that can be mixed together to fit the particular needs of different customers.

Ericsson's systems knowledge can be defined as a core competence. In general, at least three tests can be applied to identify core competences of a company (Prahalad and Hamel 1990). First, core competence provides potential access to a wide variety of markets. In the case of Ericsson, its systems competence is the key to the operators' market of mobile and stationary telephony, and to the office automation market. Second, a core competence should make a significant contribution to the perceived customer benefits of the end product. The complete solutions that Ericsson offers in the area of communications primarily imply that one takes total responsibility for the systems one delivers. This gives an obvious advantage to the customer in that it means that Ericsson will take care of all the communications problems.

Finally, a core competence is the kind of competence that is difficult for competitors to imitate. When it comes to the telecommunications systems, the complexity of the harmonization procedures for individual technologies makes imitation very difficult. Even though the major systems suppliers for public and mobile telephony networks (Alcatel, AT&T, Ericsson, Motorola, NEC, Nokia, Northern Telecom and Siemens) keep a close watch on each other, and a rival company may happen to have some of the technologies that comprise a core competence of an adversary, it will still be difficult to duplicate the intricate pattern of internal coordination and learning.

Customer divergence

Ericsson regards its main role to be that of a supplier of telecommunications systems, primarily to network operators. Although there are customers who are inclined also to assign responsibility for network operations to Ericsson, the company has no intention of becoming a telecommunications operator. This means that Ericsson does not offer to acquire a stake in a network as part of its marketing strategy.

One of the big challenges facing Ericsson as a systems supplier is regarded to be the establishment of good relationships with operators of different types, and being able to maintain these relationships for many years (*Annual Report* 1994). In particular, good relationships with large operators are considered to be crucial. Generally, one way of doing this is to apply the concept of relationship marketing (Gummesson 1995), which means that the total offering and its value for the customer is the focal point in marketing. The customer value emerges as a result of an interaction process, where the supplier and the customer constitute the main actors and other actors support (Wikström *et al.* 1994).

Thus, when it comes to Ericsson's telecommunications systems one aims at customer divergence (Figure 6.1), with the exception of systems for office automation. Historically, the traditional telecom operators, such as BT (type 1), made up the main market segment which Ericsson had penetrated, and those customers usually demanded customized systems.

As Ericsson is trying to establish relations with the operators of each of the five types, this is a sign that a customer divergence strategy is present. Besides the traditional telecom operators, the above-mentioned operator types include a number of new operators, notably in the mobile telephony part of the industry. Long-term relations require both the development of systems that are suitable for a single type, and the development of approaches that would be suitable for more than one type (*Annual Report* 1994). This means that an effort to apply a certain degree of systems standardization can be detected.

Ericsson's categorization of the network operators market follows the procedure of contractible market segmentation (Albaum *et al.* 1989). This involves a systematic screening of possible segments and leads to the elimination of less promising segments and further investigation of the more promising ones.

In the choice between the customer divergence strategy and the customer concentration strategy which implies a focus on a certain type of traditional telecom operator, the factors promoting divergence were perceived as the most important ones. The operators' market outside the traditional one shows a high growth rate, but also constantly changing conditions. As Ericsson obviously expects the five types of operators not to deviate too much from one another, the divergence strategy has been chosen. One advantage of this strategy is the fact that drastically changing market conditions will not affect Ericsson as seriously as they would if the company was dependent on fewer customer types.

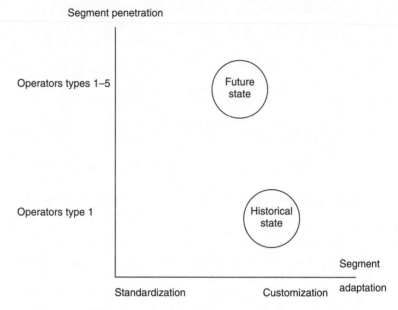

Figure 6.1 Customer divergence for Ericsson's telecommunications systems

Notes:
Type 1 Traditional telecom operators
Type 2 New operators who joined the competition as a result of deregulation
Type 3 New operators that have introduced new ways in which to confront the market
Type 4 Companies that operate specialized networks
Type 5 Companies with their bases in other industries

MANIFESTATIONS OF CUSTOMER AND GEOGRAPHIC DIVERGENCE

One of Ericsson's goals is the establishment of long-term relations with network operators of different types, including both well-known operators and new entrants. This section provides examples of how this customer divergence is reflected in Ericsson's strategy development. As the customer divergence implies entry to countries which have not been previously penetrated by Ericsson to any large degree, customer divergence also implies a certain degree of geographic divergence. The geographic divergence strategy is manifested by entry on to the markets of Germany, the USA and Japan. The establishment of customer relations in these countries and the formation of strategic alliances facilitating market entry provide examples of Ericsson's divergence strategies.

Establishment of customer relations

The way in which systems suppliers usually go about establishing relations with network operators typically assumes the following pattern. After the authority responsible for the issuing of licences in a country or region has announced its bid, Ericsson and its competitors respond and make contact with potential operators. Sometimes Ericsson appears in a given country even before the deregulation process has started:

> We were aware of the coming deregulation in Germany and in the autumn of 1988 we formulated a strategy for the market. To start with, we penetrated different possible (mobile telephony) operators and consortia that might perhaps get the D2-licence. This included 5–6 American alliances, 3–4 European and some German. . . . Around 80% of our resources were focused on the three most interesting alliances.
>
> (Tomas Mikaelsson, former Ericsson Mobile
> Telekommunikation in Germany, 23 February 1994)

Ericsson's entry into Japan followed a similar approach, and when the deregulation process in that country accelerated in 1985, Ericsson set up an office to survey the market and the country's technical development and to make personal contacts. This exploration clearly aimed at learning about the market and deciding whether a more serious commitment should be made at some later date.

Ericsson supports each of the potential operators by providing plans for their technical development, network engineering and marketing. Another important way of support is by working out methods of argumentation that may be used to persuade the responsible politicians to grant licences to the operators in question. At the beginning of this process Ericsson approaches several potential operators with standardized packages. After the agreements have been signed, the packages are customized to fit the specific needs of the operators concerned. In this phase of the relationship, the number of business relations is reduced from the initially large number with many potential operators to those that are of immediate interest, usually just one or just a few, in a given country or region.

Before Ericsson started building up its customer relations in the German public telecommunications market, an advertising campaign was launched in order to become well known on the market and to search for prospective partners. As Ericsson's market shares kept growing, despite the lack of partnership, the company continued operating on its own.

Ericsson's penetration of operators in the USA started in the early 1980s when relatively extensive transmission equipment was delivered to MCI Communications – a long-distance traffic operator. Later on, even AXE systems were delivered and the very costly customization process on the US market was initiated. This facilitated the later penetration of the interesting Bell operators.

Ericsson's business areas of Public Telecommunications and Radio Systems were together able to offer mobile telephony systems to the American customer, marking the beginning of the establishment of customer relationships. However, Ericsson's entry into this market meant building up resources in order to be able to meet the expected demand. This contrasted with Ericsson's usual entry method into a foreign market of first receiving orders and then building up resources in the country in question.

Even though the American market was not yet open to penetration at that time, in the early 1980s Ericsson had the opportunity of adapting its Scandinavian NMT standard for mobile telephony to the American AMPS standard. This development work was crucial for the future establishment of customer relations:

> We were aware of the fact that the adaptation of our system to AMPS had to be completed before the licences were distributed. The day after an operator received a licence he would invite tenders for systems, equipment and services, and some months later the selected system would be in operation.
>
> (Torbjörn Nilsson, Vice President, Ericsson Radio Systems, 23 February 1994)

Later, one way of geographical divergence on the American market was by the penetration of operators working in rural areas located between large car-intensive cities. For example, after the first system delivery to Los Angeles, Ericsson delivered another system to an operator in San Francisco in 1986. After that many operators located between these two cities would select Ericsson's systems, which meant that the two cities had been linked together. The same pattern of expansion was followed in Texas and Florida, among many other states.

Formation of strategic alliances

There is a tendency in the telecommunications industry to form strategic alliances of varying character. This tendency is valid for all groups of suppliers in this industry: equipment suppliers, systems suppliers, network operators and retailers.

Unisource is an example of a strategic alliance between network operators in international traffic. This alliance has been formed between Telia of Sweden, PTT Netherlands, the Swiss PTT and Telefonica of Spain. Other operators that have participated in the creation of alliances are BT, DBP Telekom and France Telecom, among others.

A wide range of cooperative agreements is covered by the term strategic alliance (Chakravarthy and Lorange 1991), including franchising and contract- and asset-based joint ventures. An international firm and local interests may create a new entity or partnership under local law, or international dominants may form together an entity or partnership. Some of the strategic alliances are based on formal contracts, while others are not. Some are limited to a specific project, while others are open-ended. The benefits of alliances may include access to new markets, technological know-how, the establishment of new contacts and the achievement of risk reduction. For firms that do not possess the many distinctive aspects of the necessary competence to compete successfully in their chosen sphere of business, a strategic alliance might strengthen that competence or diversify it. It can also reduce the time and the resources necessary for the acquisition of such competence.

As regards long-term joint ventures that are established through formal contracts, Chakravarthy and Lorange suggest three types of strategic alliances. The first type seeks to combine the upstream know-how of one business with the downstream forces of the prospective ally. The benefit of such an alliance would mean gaining insight and access to the partner's technological and manufacturing know-how or benefiting from the partner's established position on the market. The second type of alliance combines the downstream activities of the two cooperating firms. It may call for the merging of their product lines and sales channels. The alliance may be able to offer a broader product line to customers of both parents. Finally, the third type of strategic alliance means a combination of operational capabilities of the two partners in order to exploit the economies of scale, perhaps also covering the joint effort invested in research and development activities. After this presentation Chakravarthy and Lorange conclude that the actual types of strategic alliances formed in reality are usually of a mixed type.

Ericsson also participates in the formation of strategic alliances. The following quotation expresses the company's intentions in this respect:

Ericsson is strong enough to be able to continue as an independent company with its own core products. We shall become even better in areas where we have our real strength. At the same time, we must realize that we cannot do everything by ourselves. Through co-operation in various areas, we are achieving efficiency and the necessary volumes of business required to support continued development work.

(CEO Björn Svedberg, *Annual Report* 1986)

The willingness to form strategic alliances, in the areas in which they are considered relevant and desirable, seems to have been even more emphasized after 1986. In the *Annual Report* of 1994, cooperation with other companies was regarded to be a very important policy aspect as regards future development. The following list provides examples of Ericsson's long-term joint ventures:

- In the early 1970s Ericsson owned a part of the American telecommunications company Northern Electric, and the public AKE exchange (a precursor of the AXE exchange) was sold in the USA by Northern Electric.
- In 1980 Ericsson and the American Atlantic Richfield company formed Anaconda-Ericsson, based on equal shares. Atlantic Richfield contributed mainly by providing its cable activities and a small private branch exchange for office use.
- A supply agreement with Honeywell of the USA was entered into in 1983, and this covered the resale of communications systems for offices through Honeywell's marketing organization.
- A development company was formed together with Honeywell in 1983 for the adaptation of Ericsson's communications systems to American standards and for further development of the systems.
- In 1989 Ericsson and General Electric formed Ericsson GE Mobile Communications. One of the advantages to Ericsson was that GE's sales and service organization was to be used.
- Ericsson and Matra of France signed an agreement in the early 1990s to develop and market GSM systems for mobile telephony in Europe.
- Ericsson participated as one of the three members making up the Flexnode consortium that was selected in 1990 to deliver transmission equipment to DBP Telekom in Germany.

172

- In the early 1990s Ericsson started a mobile telephony joint venture with Toshiba in Japan. This new company will instal, maintain and service the networks of the Digital Phone Group companies in Japan, following the Japanese digital cellular standard.

Ericsson GE Mobile Communications is a long-term joint venture which might be classified into more than one of the Chakravarthy and Lorange's types. Ericsson held 60 per cent and GE 40 per cent of the shares initially, and later Ericsson bought another 20 per cent. The business mission of this joint venture company was expressed as follows:

> To offer advanced products, systems and services for cellular mobile telephony systems in the U.S.A. and Canada, and for mobile communications and mobile telephones globally.
>
> (Lars Ramqvist, Radio Communications business area of
> Ericsson, *Annual Report* 1989)

Since the company is helping Ericsson to build up its market knowledge, it may be classified into the first type of strategic alliance. The two partners also share the technological know-how, and the joint venture company has established a development centre for the management of digital mobile telephony. This implies also a type three strategic alliance.

REFERENCES

Abell, D. (1980) *Defining the Business: The Starting Point of Strategic Planning*, Englewood Cliffs, NJ: Prentice-Hall International.

Abell, D. and Hammond, J. (1979) *Strategic Market Planning: Problems and Analytical Approaches*, Englewood Cliffs, NJ: Prentice-Hall International.

Albaum, G., Dowd, L., Duerr, E. and Strandskov, J. (1989) *International Marketing and Export Management*, Wokingham: Addison-Wesley.

Andrews, K. (1971) *The Concept of Corporate Strategy*, Homewood, Ill.: Dow Jones-Irwin.

Ansoff, I. (1965) *Corporate Strategy*, New York: McGraw-Hill.

Attman, A., Kuuse, J. and Olsson, U. (1977a) *The Pioneering Years' Struggle for Concessions Crises, 1876–1932*, L.M. Ericsson 100 years, vol. 1, Stockholm: Interbook Publishing.

—— (1977b) *Rescue, Reconstruction, Worldwide Enterprise, 1932–1976*, L.M. Ericsson 100 years, vol. 2, Stockholm: Interbook Publishing.

—— (1977c) *Evolution of the Technology, 1876–1976*, L.M. Ericsson 100 years, vol. 3, Stockholm: Interbook Publishing.

Boddewyn, J., Soehl, R. and Picard, J. (1986) 'Standardization in international marketing: is Ted Levitt in fact right?', *Business Horizons*, November–December: 69–75.

Bonoma, T. and Shapiro, B. (1983) *Segmenting the Industrial Market*, Lexington, MA: Lexington Books.

Bourgeois III, L. (1980) 'Strategy and environment: a conceptual integration', *Academy of Management Review*, 5: 25–39.

Brandes, O. and Brege, S. (1990) *Market Leadership* [in Swedish], Malmö, Sweden: Liber.

Buzzell, R. (1968) 'Can you standardize multinational marketing?', *Harvard Business Review*, November–December: 102–13.

Buzzell, R., Gale, B. and Sultan, R. (1975) 'Market share: a key to profitability', *Harvard Business Review*, 1: 97–106.

Caves R. and Pugel, T. (1980) *Intra-industry Differences in Conduct and Performance: Viable Strategies in the U.S. Manufacturing Industries*, monograph, New York University.

Chakravarthy, B. and Lorange, P. (1991) *Managing the Strategy Process*, Englewood Cliffs, NJ: Prentice-Hall International.

174

REFERENCES

Chandler, A. (1962) *Strategy and Structure: Chapters in the History of American Enterprise*, Cambridge, MA: MIT Press.

Chrisman, J., Hofer, C. and Boulton, W. (1988) 'Toward a system for classifying business strategies', *Academy of Management Review*, 3: 413–28.

Dess, G. and Davis, P. (1984) 'Porter's generic strategies as determinants of strategic group membership and organizational performance', *Academy of Management Journal*, 27: 467–88.

Douglas, S. and Wind, Y. (1987) 'The myth of globalization', *Columbia Journal of World Business*, Winter: 19–29.

Doz, Y. (1986) 'Government policies and global industries', in M. Porter (ed.), *Competition in Global Industries*, Boston, MA: Harvard Business School Press.

Flodhammar, Å. (1977) *Industrial Marketing Segmentation*, dissertation in Swedish, Linköping University, Linköping, Sweden.

Galbraith, C. and Schendel, D. (1983) 'An empirical analysis of strategy types', *Strategic Management Journal*, 4: 153–73.

Ginsberg, A. and Venkatraman, N. (1985) 'Contingency perspectives of organizational strategy: a critical review of the empirical research', *Academy of Management Review*, 10: 421–34.

Glete, J. (1983) *ASEA During 100 Years, 1883–1983: A Study of the Organizational, Technical and Financial Development of a Large Company* [in Swedish], Stockholm: Stenströms.

Gorringe, M. and Hartikainen, M. (1991) *The Market for Large Company Exchanges*, MBA essay in Swedish, Stockholm University, Stockholm.

Gummesson, E. (1995) *Relationship Marketing: from 4 Ps to 30 Rs* [in Swedish], Malmö: Liber-Hermods.

Hambrick, D. (1983) 'Some tests of the effectiveness and functional attributes of Miles and Snow's strategic types', *Academy of Management Journal*, 26: 5–26.

Hambrick, D. and Lei, D. (1985) 'Toward an empirical prioritization of contingency variables for business strategy', *Academy of Management Journal*, 28: 763–88.

Hamel, G. and Prahalad, C. (1985) 'Do you really have a global strategy?', *Harvard Business Review*, July–August: 139–48.

Hatten, K. and Schendel, D. (1977) 'Heterogeneity within an industry', *Journal of Industrial Economics*: 97–113.

Hatten, K., Schendel, D. and Cooper, A. (1978) 'A strategic model for the U.S. brewing industry: 1952–1971', *Academy of Management Journal*, 21: 592–610.

Henderson, B. (1979) *Henderson on Corporate Strategy*, Cambridge, MA: Abt. Books.

Hill, C. (1988) 'Differentiation versus low cost or differentiation and low cost: a contingency framework', *Academy of Management Review*, 13: 401–12.

Hofer, C. (1975) 'Toward a contingency theory of business strategy', *Academy of Management Journal*, 18: 784–810.

Hofer, C. and Schendel, D. (1978) *Strategy Formulation: Analytical Concepts*, St. Paul, Minnesota: West.

Humes, S. (1993) *Managing the Multinational: Confronting the Global–Local Dilemma*, Hemel Hempstead: Prentice-Hall International.

Hunt, M. (1972) *Competition in the Major Home Appliance Industry 1960–1970*, Cambridge, MA: Harvard University.

Jain, S. (1989) 'Standardization of international marketing strategy: some research hypotheses', *Journal of Marketing*, 53: 70–9.

Johnson, G. and Scholes, K. (1993) *Exploring Corporate Strategy*, Hemel Hempstead: Prentice-Hall.

Jolly, V. (1988) 'Global competitive strategies,' in C. Snow (ed.), *Strategy, Organization Design and Human Resource Management*, Greenwich, CT: JAI Press.

Keegan, N. (1969) 'Multinational product planning: strategic alternatives', *Journal of Marketing*, January: 58–62.

Kotler, P. (1991) *Marketing Management*, Englewood Cliffs, NJ: Prentice-Hall.

Lahti, A. (1983) *Strategy and Performance of a Firm: An Empirical Investigation in the Knitwear Industry in Finland, 1969–81*, Helsinki: Helsinki School of Economics.

Levitt, T. (1983) 'The globalization of markets', *Harvard Business Review*, May–June: 99–102.

Lorange, P. (1980) *Corporate Planning: An Executive Viewpoint*, Englewood Cliffs, NJ: Prentice-Hall International.

McGee, J. and Thomas, H. (1986) 'Strategic groups: theory, research and taxonomy', *Strategic Management Journal*, 7: 141–60.

Miles, R. and Snow, C. (1978) *Organizational Strategy, Structure and Process*, New York: McGraw-Hill.

Miller, D. (1987) 'The structural and environmental correlates of business strategy', *Strategic Management Journal*, 8: 55–76.

Miller, D. (1988) 'Relating Porter's business strategies to environment and structure: analysis and performance implications', *Academy of Management Journal*, 31: 280–308.

Mintzberg, H. and Waters, J. (1985) 'Of strategies, deliberate and emergent', *Strategic Management Journal*, 6: 257–72.

Morrison, A. and Roth, K. (1992) 'A taxonomy of business-level strategies in global industries', *Strategic Management Journal*, 13: 399–418.

Newman, H. (1978) 'Strategic groups and the structure/performance relationship', *Review of Economics and Statistics*, 60: 417–27.

Pehrsson, A. (1985) *Strategic Planning and Environmental Judgements: The Performance in S.B.U. Organized Industrial Groups*, dissertation, Linköping University, Linköping, Sweden.

Pehrsson, A. (1988) *Strategic Planning: Tools for Market Orientation and Long Term Survival* [in Swedish], Lund: Studentlitteratur.

Pehrsson, A. (1990) 'Strategic groups in international competition', *Scandinavian Journal of Management*, 6: 109–24.

Pehrsson, A. (1991) *International Business Strategies* [in Swedish], Malmö: Liber.

Pehrsson, A. (1993) 'A contingency perspective of strategy choice problems: experiences of Swedish companies in Germany', *Journal of Strategic Change*, March–April: 89–101.

Pehrsson, A. (1995a) 'Strategic states and performance: Swedish companies in Germany', *Journal of Strategic Change*, 4: 229–37.

176

Pehrsson, A. (1995b) 'International product strategies: an exploratory study', *Scandinavian Journal of Management*, 11: 237–49.

Persson, L. (1990) *A New Paradigm for Description and Evaluation of Competitive Relations* [compendium in Swedish], Stockholm University.

Porter, M. (1973) *Consumer Behavior, Retail Power and Manufacturer Strategy in Consumer Goods Industries*, Cambridge, MA: Harvard University.

Porter, M. (1980) *Competitive Strategy*, New York: The Free Press.

Porter, M. (1986) *Competition in Global Industries*, Boston, MA: Harvard Business School Press.

Prahalad, C. and Doz, Y. (1987) *The Multinational Mission*, New York: The Free Press.

Prahalad, C. and Hamel, G. (1990) 'The core competence of the corporation', *Harvard Business Review*, May–June.

Primeaux, W. (1985) 'A method for determining strategic groups and life cycle stages in an industry', in H. Thomas and D. Gardner (eds), *Strategic Marketing and Management*, Chichester: Wiley.

Quelch, J. and Hoff, E. (1986) 'Customizing global marketing', *Harvard Business Review*, May–June: 59–68.

Rumelt, R. (1980) 'The evaluation of business strategy', in W. Glueck (ed.), *Business Policy and Strategic Management*, Maidenhead: McGraw-Hill.

Rumelt, R. (1982) 'Diversification strategy and profitability', *Strategic Management Journal*, 4: 359–69.

Samiee, S. and Roth, K. (1992) 'The influence of global marketing standardization on performance', *Journal of Marketing*, April: 1–17.

Sölvell, Ö., Zander, I. and Porter, M. (1991) *Advantage Sweden*, Stockholm: Norstedts.

Sorenson, R. and Wiechmann, U. (1975) 'How multinationals view marketing standardization', *Harvard Business Review*, May–June: 38–54.

Steiner, G. (1979a) *Strategic Planning*, New York: The Free Press.

—— (1979b) 'Contingency theories of strategy and strategic management', in D. Schendel and C. Hofer (eds), *Strategic Management: A New View of Business Policy and Planning*, Boston: Little, Brown.

Tall, M. (1995) *Vertical Integration on the Mobile Telephony Market*, MBA essay in Swedish, School of Business, Stockholm University.

Thompson, J. (1967) *Organizations in Action*, London: McGraw-Hill.

Toyne, B. and Walters, P. (1989) *Global Marketing Management: A Strategic Perspective*, Needham, MA: Allyn and Bacon.

Usunier, J. (1993) *International Marketing: A Cultural Approach*, Hemel Hempstead: Prentice-Hall International.

Venkatraman, N. and Ramanujam, V. (1986) 'Measurement of business performance in strategy research: a comparison of approaches', *Academy of Management Review*, 4: 801–14.

Walters, P. (1986) 'International marketing policy: a discussion of the standardization construct and its relevance for corporate policy', *Journal of International Business Studies*, summer: 55–69.

Wikström, S., Normann, R., Anell, B., Ekvall, G., Forslin, J. and Skärvad, P.H. (1994) *Knowledge and Value*, London: Routledge.

SECONDARY INFORMATION

Annual Report of Allgon (1993)

Annual Report of Ericsson (1982–94), and product brochures.

Annual Report of Telia Mobitel (1993).

'World champion in mobile and personal telephones' [in Swedish] (1992) *Affärsvärlden*, 25 April.

'Datatronic negotiates about Ericsson's problems' [in Swedish] (1985) *Dagens Industri*, 2 September.

'Robotics industry market data' (1987) Dataquest, Inc., October.

'The office of the future' [internal market analysis in Swedish] (1981) Ericsson Information Systems AB, Stockholm.

'Strategic planning in Ericsson' [internal paper in Swedish] (1983) Ericsson's Group Staff of Strategic Planning, Stockholm, November.

'We only have one Swedish robot manufacturer' [in Swedish] (1986a) *Modern Produktion*, 3.

'In the shadow of ASEA' [in Swedish] (1986b) *Modern Produktion*, 6.

Jahrbuch 1989 [Annual review 1989] (1989) Schwedische Handelskammer in der B.R.D., Düsseldorf.

'EIS sells to a Norwegian company' [in Swedish] (1987) *Svenska Dagbladet*, 21 October.

'Nokia buys a data division' [in Swedish] (1988) *Svenska Dagbladet*, 21 January.

'Now Björn Svedberg can rest' [in Swedish] (1989) *Svenska Dagbladet*, 27 August.

The Robotics Technology Makes Swedish Industry Even Better [in Swedish] (1987) Swedish Industrial Robot Association.

Teldok Info [in Swedish] (1994) Telia AB, Stockholm, May.

The Teldok Yearbook 1994 (1994) Telia AB, Stockholm.

'The telecommunications war: Ericsson takes its own way' [in Swedish] (1983a) *Veckans Affärer*, 3 February.

'Ericsson into the U.S. with a record issue' [in Swedish] (1983b) *Veckans Affärer*, 17 February.

'Ericsson has to earn another billion' [in Swedish] (1984) *Veckans Affärer*, 13 December.

'Employment stop and significant rationalizations at the E.I.S.' [in Swedish] (1985a) *Veckans Affärer*, 21 February.

'After the shock in 1984: AXE returns into focus' [in Swedish] (1985b) *Veckans Affärer*, 18 April.

'Now Ericsson must show financial results' [in Swedish] (1987) *Veckans Affärer*, 21 May.

'It certainly has pained . . . ' [in Swedish] (1988) *Veckans Affärer*, 14.

Übersicht zugelassener Telekommunikationssysteme [in German] (1991) Zentralamt für Zulassungen im Fernmeldewesen, 31 March.

INDEX

179